All the Music of the Bible

All the Music of the Bible

■ ■ ■

Herbert Lockyer Jr.

HENDRICKSON PUBLISHERS

ALL THE MUSIC OF THE BIBLE
© 2004 Herbert Lockyer Jr.

Hendrickson Publishers, Inc.
P. O. Box 3473
Peabody, Massachusetts 01961–3473

ISBN: 1-56563-540-X cloth
ISBN: 1-56563-531-0 paper

First Printing—July 2004

Printed in the United States of America

Various Bible versions are used in this book. Scripture quotations marked KJV are from the KING JAMES VERSION OF THE BIBLE. Quotations marked NIV are from the HOLY BIBLE, NEW INTERNATIONAL VERSION®—©1973, 1978, 1984 by International Bible Society. Used by permission of Zondervan Publishing House. All rights reserved. Quotations marked NASB are taken from the NEW AMERICAN STANDARD BIBLE, ©1977, The Lockman Foundation. Quotations marked NKJV are taken from the THE HOLY BIBLE, NEW KING JAMES VERSION, ©1982, Thomas Nelson, Inc. Quotations marked NRSV are taken from the NEW REVISED STANDARD VERSION, ©1989 by the Division of Christian Education of the National Council of the Churches of Christ in the United States of America. Used by permission. All rights reserved. Quotations marked NLT are taken from the HOLY BIBLE, NEW LIVING TRANSLATION, copyright ©1996 by Tyndale Charitable Trust. Used by permission of Tyndale House Publishers. Quotations marked YLT are taken from YOUNG'S LITERAL TRANSLATION OF THE HOLY BIBLE by Robert Young. Quotations marked JB are taken from The Jerusalem Bible Reader's Edition, copyright ©1968, Doubleday. Quotations marked NJPS are taken from TANAKH, THE HOLY SCRIPTURES ©1985, The Jewish Publication Society.

Library of Congress Cataloging-in-Publication Data

Lockyer, Herbert, Jr.
    All the music of the Bible : an exploration of musical expression in scripture and church hymnody / Herbert Lockyer Jr.
      p. cm.
    Includes bibliographical references and index.
    ISBN: 1-56563-540-X (alk. paper) — ISBN: 1-56563-531-0 (pbk. : alk. paper)
  1. Music in the Bible. 2. Music—Religious aspects—Christianity. I. Title.
    ML 166.L53 2004
    781.71'009—dc22
                            2004009661

Contents

Foreword

IN 1969, Herbert Lockyer Sr. wrote:

> If, to the true musician, all nature carries the sound and melody of music—the singing of the birds, the bubbling of a brook, the rustling of leaves, the rolling waves of the sea, and peals of thunder—where could such an appreciation of rhythmic expression come from save from Him who made humans? Here we have an aspect of the divine being that we are apt to neglect. All melody, harmony, and joyful praises spring from Him who, as the happy God, created humans to be like Himself. In the New Testament, the Greek word *makarios* is translated "blessed" or "happy." Paul used the word in Acts 26:2 to describe himself as he stood before Agrippa. In 1 Tim. 1:11 and 6:15, he refers to God as the blessed or happy one.
>
> Is this not why the Bible is such a happy book and has so much to say about vocal and instrumental music? It abounds in praise and reverberates with the music of heaven. Glance over its sacred pages, and you will find that its psalms outweigh its sighs. Passages speaking of war, suffering, sorrow, strife, fears, and of all that destroys are few compared with the multitude of references to praise, joy, singing, happiness, gladness, and peace. No matter where you turn in the Bible, melody predominates over misery and songs over sobs. Happy were the people who had a happy God as their Lord and praised Him by lips, lute, and lyre. Melody is a natural mode of uttering the grateful emotions of the mind, a faculty conferred on humans by their creator for that very purpose. This is why we are called upon by prophets and psalmists to "sing and give praise," both with and without instruments of music.[1]

As we will see, music, both vocal and instrumental, was well culti-vated among the Hebrews, the New Testament Christians, and the Christian church through the centuries. A cursory glance at the Old Testament reveals how God's ancient people were devoted to the study and practice of music, which holds a unique place in the historical and prophetic books, as well as the Psalter. While it may be difficult to fully identify some items in the vocabulary of musical terms, the range of emotions expressed by Hebrew music was anything but limited. Such music was capable of expressing a great variety of moods and feelings or the broadly marked antitheses of joy and sorrow, hope and fear, faith and doubt. In fact, every shade and quality of sentiment are found in the wealth of songs and psalms and in the diverse melodies of a people who ranked their music highly in divine service.

An as introduction to the study before us, we have the magnificent concert held on the shores of the Red Sea after Israel had passed over in Exod. 15:1–20. "The words were adapted to the occasion," says Dr. Her-bert Lockyer Sr., "the music to the words; the performers to the music. There we behold Moses leading the bolder, rougher notes of manly voices. Here, Miriam, the prophetess, his sister, in sweet accord, blend-ing the softer harmony of female strains of the timbrel, in praises of their great Deliverer."[2] What a sight and sound that must have been, a fore-gleam of the host of redeemed choristers that John describes as singing and playing harps on the shores of the new Jerusalem. "They held harps given them by God and sang the song of Moses the servant of God and the song of the Lamb" (Rev. 15:2b–3 NIV).

I wish to see all arts, principally music, in the service of Him who gave and created them. Music is a fair and glorious gift of God. I would not for the world forego my humble share of music. Sing-ers are never sorrowful, but are merry, and smile through their troubles in song. Music makes people kinder, gentler, more staid and reasonable. . . . I am strongly persuaded that after theology, there is no art that can be placed on a level with music; for besides theology, music is the only art capable of affording peace and joy of the heart. . . . the devil flees before the sound of music almost as much as before the Word of God.[3]

Preface
The Origin of Music

*Music is well said to be the speech of angels; in fact, nothing among the utter-
ance allowed to [humans] is felt to be so divine. It brings us near to the infinite.*
—Thomas Carlyle

MUSIC. What is this mystery that gives flight to the imagination, touches
the deepest emotions, and speaks to the soul? From poets and mystics to
saints and sinners, from antiquity to the immediacy of each breath we
take, music communicates when words cannot. Since the dawn of creation, artists have been exploring the many ways in which music communicates beyond words. Indeed, music is a language unto itself, a
language born in the heart of God countless ages before creation.

But why study all the music of the Bible? Why do we create music?
How does listening to music affect the soul? How do we, mere humans,
collaborate with the Holy Spirit to combine notes and tones into melodies and songs that reflect what cannot be said by words alone? How
can we put the utterances of our soul on paper and into a form?

These are the questions that a study of all the music of the Bible
will consider. This book explores how people throughout time and
across cultures have done just that. We will look at how ordinary
people responded to God's call to extraordinary work, and in so doing,
transcended the limitations of their own humanity to express themselves with the language of angels.

Part 1 will explore ancient songs of the Old Testament. In Part 2, we
will consider the Hebrew poetry of David, Isaiah, and Solomon. New

Testament songs and modern hymnody are the concern of Part 3. Finally, we will spend a few moments with my father's notes on music in Part 4.

As Herbert Lockyer's son, I listened to my father preach and teach well beyond the four score years of an average lifetime. My father lived to the age of 98 and actively continued to study and teach the Word of God well into his eighties. I treasure the length of his years on earth and the wealth of wisdom I learned from this faithful man of God. His three essays are included in this book in honor of his remarkable ability to see beyond the text to the spiritual meaning deep within—and communicate that meaning to others. The first is a mediation, "Instrument of Ten Strings," I heard my father use many times in his teaching and preaching. The second is a brief study of "Nebuchadnezzar's Orchestra," a study which demonstrates how magnificent music must have been in Biblical times. And the third is a story I heard my father tell many times.

In the opening passage of his lilting motet *"Der Geist hilft unser Schwachheit auf,"* J.S. Bach immortalized the idea of transcendent expression by setting the German translation of Rom. 8:26 to music.

Der Geist hilft unser Schwachheit auf,
> *The Spirit helps us in our weakness,*

denn wir wissen nicht,
> *since, when we do not know*

was wir beten sollen, wie sichs gebühret;
> *what we should pray for,*

sondern der Geist selbst vertritt uns aufs
> *then the Spirit personally makes our petition for us*

beste mit unaussprechlichem Seufzen
> *in sighs that cannot be put into words.*

From Moses and Miriam to Paul and Silas to Jan Hus and John Calvin, music is as integrated into the lives and faith of the people of God as prayer, praise, and worship. This study of *All the Music of the Bible* invites you to walk through the pages of Scripture and hymnody and draw near to the Infinite as you journey into the heart of the divine.

PART 1

■   ■   ■

Music of the Ancients

1

Ancient Music

The one who sings, prays twice. —Saint Augustine

HUMAN HISTORY is rich with music, though music predates any *human* musical expression. From the beginning of time, music has filled the world. The moment God separated the land from the seas and filled the skies with birds, music was born. A walk in the woods is a symphony of sound. A visit to the ocean's shore is an opportunity to hear again the percussion of a world alive with sound.

With the music of nature often silenced in our modern culture, we are, nonetheless, both serenaded and bombarded with music, constantly. In our homes and cars, at the grocery store, in elevators and offices, even on the streets, we hear a diversity of sound and rhythm that would have mystified primitive human beings. Music today may bring tears or energize our bodies. Music may tell a tale or become a prayer. But this diversity of musical expression and the many venues in which we enjoy it is a recent development in the history of music.

In ancient times, music and ritual were inseparable. Through the pounding of drums before a hunt or celebrations of a plentiful harvest, music was integral to the life of primitive tribes. Across time and space, cultures and geography, music and life are inseparable—and have been since music was born in the heart of God. Music *affects* us, deeply, powerfully, and prophetically.

"There is something about human beings that needs to make music, something that insists on song," writes Don E. Saliers. "The act of singing together is deeply and indelibly human. When we sing, words are given greater range and power than when we speak."[1]

To study the music of the ancient people who eventually became the Israelites is to acknowledge the vital, essential role music has played in the drama of the human race. Though scholarly research and archeological finds confirm the significance of music in ancient times and we know with certainty the need and desire of the people of God to express love and praise to their Creator, we know almost nothing of how the ancient music actually *sounded*. Much of the history of Hebrew music eludes musical scholars to this day. We have no knowledge of the ancient Hebrew scales, their methods of tuning instruments, or the integration of the human voice with instrumentation.

Ancient Music

The term "ancient music" has been used by historians to represent music up to 450 A.D. and includes the cultures of ancient Greece and the first few centuries of the Christian church. Our knowledge of music from this time is so limited, quite simply, because history was passed from generation to generation orally, by rote repetition of verse, poetry, and song. Few attempts were made by ancient cultures to preserve music or history by writing it down.

However, there are rare exceptions. In the 1950's, an archeological dig in Syria uncovered a set of clay tablets with characters written in the ancient Hurrian language, a language used by citizens of the city of Ugarit in Mesopotamia as early as the third millennium or earlier. The tablets, measuring seven and a half inches long by three inches high, date back to approximately 1400 B.C. Remarkably, the tablets include detailed performance instructions for a singer accompanied by a harpist and contain a hymn to the goddess Nikal.[2] A limited understanding of the Hurrian language has resulted in only one translated phrase of the hymn: "Thou [the goddess] lovest them in [thy] heart." Love was expressed in song at least five thousand years ago.

The music of ancient Greece was inseparable from poetry, dancing, and theatre, with the principal instrument being the human voice. Yet the music of this ancient civilization was almost entirely monophonic, consisting of a single melody without a contrasting line or harmony. In the case of the "Hurrian Hymn to Nikal," the harpist most likely played the same line the singer sang, perhaps with slight improvisations.

We also know from the work of scholars that in the sixth century B.C., choral music was utilized in drama with instruments such as the aulos, a type of oboe. After the fall of Athens in 404 B.C., an anti-intellectual reaction took place and gave birth to the professional musician who employed more elaborate melody and rhythms in music composition and performance.

Early Christians undoubtedly took their cue from the ancient Greeks by composing monophonic music. As the Christian faith spread throughout the world, it incorporated the styles, instrumentation, and rhythms of many indigenous cultures as the early disciples of Christ carried the message of the one true and holy God into foreign lands. But jumping ahead to the time of Christ and the early Christian church is moving ahead much too quickly. To look at *All the Music of the Bible* is first to look at Abram, the patriarch of the Hebrew people.

The Beginnings of a Nation

The history of the Israelites as recorded in the Old Testament reveals a landscape of physical, mental, and emotional difficulties, a series of challenges that became the story of humans at our best and our worst. Abram, eventually renamed Abraham (Gen. 17:5), was the patriarch of the Hebrew people. Abram was an old man of seventy-five years when he heard the call of God, instructing Abram to move his entire family and all of his possessions to Canaan, the chosen land.

In a magnificent showing of faith, Abraham left all that was familiar to lead his clan to Canaan (ca. 2090 B.C.), beginning the saga of God's chosen people chronicled in the Old Testament. Few pieces of literature rival these adventures for the drama and intrigue, romance and betrayals, hope and despair that characterized this journey into the unknown. Faith in God eroded with the fickleness of human emotions as the wandering clan confronted difficulties for which they were unprepared. Hunger, thirst, boredom, fear, jealousy, and even a longing for the "good old days" of enslavement were all part of the human experience God used to prepare them for the promised land, a land which mirrored the inconsistencies of the Abrahamic clan.

This land of plenty and want flowed "with milk and honey" (Num. 13:27), as well as including vast wilderness areas void of vegetation. The diversity of the land itself symbolized both the faithful presence and seeming absence of this powerful God, known to the wandering tribe only as "Yahweh."

A harsh climate, lack of many natural resources, and rugged terrain might seem an unlikely place for Yahweh to send His chosen people. An area of land measuring roughly 10,330 square miles, approximately the size of the state of Maryland, the territory to which Yahweh was leading His chosen people, was an area strategic for sea trade and commerce, a region forming the only intercontinental land bridge linking Asia and Europe with Africa, linking the Atlantic with the Indian Ocean by way of the Red Sea and the Mediterranean.

Not only was this land a strategic region geographically, but the difficulties the land presented forced the Israelites to rely on Yahweh for survival, demanding the trust and obedience Yahweh desired from the children of Israel. The journey that began the story of Abraham and Sarah and a fledgling nation is both spiritual and geographic, and the significance of music is integral to both.

Ancient Form and Function

The emphasis on music in the Old Testament offers assurance that music played an important part in the Hebrews' worship of Yahweh. References to music, praise, and singing in the Bible outnumber references to prayer and praying almost 2 to 1; in other words, twice as many biblical passages mention music as do prayer! Obviously, the Word of God has something to say about the importance of music in the life of those who seek to know God. Writing in the fourth century, Saint Augustine observed, "Apart from those moments when the scriptures are being read or a sermon is preached, when . . . praying aloud or . . . speaking prayer, is there any time when the faithful are not singing?"

The most important form of music in ancient Hebrew life was the song; the essential purpose of instrumental music was to underlie a song's thought, to make the sung word more easily understood. It is striking to discover that the use of musical instruments is especially mentioned in the early texts of the Old Testament, relatively little in the more recent, and not at all in the New Testament until the Revelation of John. This pattern is likely a corollary to the development of musical instruments themselves. As their potential grew and numbers increased, instrumental sounds became fuller and more pleasant. Instruments acquired a language of their own, independent of the spoken word, and instrumental music became self-sufficient, an expression alongside the spoken word.

Hebrews sang in unison without need of harmony or counterpoint. The effectiveness of the music depended on the number of singers and the size of the participating orchestra. The orchestra sometimes played instrumental interludes as indicated by the word *selah* (louder playing or "forte"), which appears more than seventy times in Psalms.

This emphasis is illustrated wonderfully in 1 Chr. 25 where the temple chorus and orchestra, numbering several thousand, were divided into twenty-four sections and trained and conducted by the sons of Asaph, Heman, and Jeduthun. No doubt the music inspired the worshippers as they remembered Yahweh's blessings during very difficult times.

In Israel, as elsewhere, no popular or family feast passed without music. Singing and dancing is present when sending loved ones off on a journey to another land. When Jacob sneaks away from his father-in-law, Laban follows him asking, "Why did you flee away secretly, and steal away from me, and not tell me; for I might have sent you away with joy and songs, with timbrel and harp?" (Gen. 31:27 NKJV).

The court and nobility engaged or "owned" singers, both men and women, while commoners feasted with singing to the harp and tambourine as well. When these feasts drew the Israelites into drunkenness and debauchery, the prophets used music as an example of luxury and dissoluteness in their prophecies.

Music also played a role in the act of prophesying itself. Elisha asked for music one day, and while a harpist played "the hand of the LORD came upon him [Elisha]" (2 Kgs. 3:15 NKJV). At times of mourning, at funerals and burials, music was played, perhaps intended to drive away evil spirits. For example, we know when David played his harp for Saul, a tormented Saul was refreshed and made well:

> David would take a harp and play it with his hand. Then Saul would become refreshed and well, and the distressing spirit would depart from him. (1 Sam. 16:23 NKJV)

Songs of the Targum

The historical and cultural significance of music in the life of the ancient people of God is underscored by a pivotal development. During the sixth and fifth centuries B.C., the Hebrew people were taken into captivity by the Babylonians and forbidden from speaking, singing or worshipping in Hebrew. The dominant language spoken by the Babylonian captors was Aramaic, and Aramaic became the official language of the Persian Empire. Their grief is captured in Ps. 137:

> By the rivers of Babylon,
> There we sat down, yea, we wept
> When we remembered Zion.
>
> We hung our harps
> Upon the willows in the midst of it.
>
> For there those who carried us away captive asked of us a
>   song,
> And those who plundered us requested mirth,
> Saying, "Sing us one of the songs of Zion!"
>
> How shall we sing the LORD's song
> In a foreign land?
>
> If I forget you, O Jerusalem,
> Let my right hand forget its skill!
>
> If I do not remember you,
> Let my tongue cling to the roof of my mouth—
> If I do not exalt Jerusalem above my chief joy.
> (Ps. 137:1–6 NKJV)

Assyrian Captives (perhaps Northern Israelites) Playing Harps[3]
Figure 1.1 from a bas-relief in the British Museum

Afraid of losing their songs along with their language, Ezra and the Hebrew scribes translated and paraphrased Hebrew songs and Scriptures into Aramaic, and the translated documents became known as the Targum, meaning "the translation." Some of the songs in the Targum are the same texts we find in the Hebrew Old Testament today. That these sacred texts are recorded in both languages and survived throughout centuries demonstrates the significance these songs played in the memory and worship of Israel. By the time of Christ, Aramaic had become the common language of Palestine, and was, in fact, the language Jesus himself spoke. During synagogue services of His time, one verse of the Hebrew text would be read, followed by a translation and explanation in Aramaic; by the second or third century A.D., only the Aramaic translation was read.

Unlike the Scriptures themselves, the Targum became a depository of commentary *in addition to* the translated sacred texts. The scribes who translated the texts would include observations, explanations, and historical notes, providing modern scholars with valuable insights and information about the religious life and daily practices of the Israelites.

In the earliest Targum, several songs are highlighted as particularly meaningful. Tradition attributes the first song to Adam, who rejoiced when his sins were forgiven. According to the story, when the Sabbath came, he put a covering on his lips and sang a psalm for the Sabbath day, though the actual song is lost and goes unrecorded in the translation.

Three songs of the Exodus follow. Moses led the children of Israel in singing when the Lord divided the Red Sea for them to pass (Exod. 15:1–21), and Israel sang again when Yahweh revealed the well of water at Beer (Num. 21:16–18). At the end of his life, Moses sang an exhortation to the house of Israel (Deut. 32:1–43). Again, though we don't know what the songs themselves actually *sounded* like, the texts of the songs follow a consistent theme and one which ultimately becomes one of the major themes of the Bible itself: that of deliverance.

The Targum goes on to note the song of Joshua, a song of conquest following the fight at Gibeon; the Scriptures record that the sun and moon stood still for thirty-six hours (Josh. 10:12–13). The Targum includes the subsequent songs and stories told through music of Israelite judges, prophets, and kings. Barak and Deborah sang the day the LORD delivered Sisera and his army into the hands of the children of Israel (Jdg. 5:1–31). Hannah sang when LORD gave her a son, Samuel (1 Sam. 2:1–10). David, the king of Israel, sang of the wonders the LORD had done for him and by the spirit of prophecy (2 Sam. 22:1–51). Solomon, his son and heir, also sang before Jehovah (see Song of Songs). Finally, the Targum celebrates Isaiah's restoration song in which he promises the captive Jews in Babylon that they shall sing again as though they were home in Israel on a festival night (Isa. 30:29–33).

What becomes clear when reading through these familiar stories of the Old Testament, looking specifically at what events brought forth songs of response, is that music was a primary tool of preserving the history of the chosen people of God. Long before the Holy Scriptures were committed to paper by scribes, the stories themselves were preserved by what scholars and historians call "oral tradition," one generation telling the stories over and over to the next generation. What easier way to remember than putting those stories to music? The songs of the Old Testament tell us again and again that Yahweh, the one true and Holy Lord, delivers the faithful. Whatever the anguish of His people, whether from oppression, sorrow, injustice, want or need, God is with His people in a timeless covenant of love and redemption. Although we will examine many of these ancient texts more thoroughly in the coming chapters, what is worthy to note is the common melody that flows throughout all the music born in ancient times and places. That melody is one of divine love, calling, pursuing, delivering, and redeeming a chosen people. (For a list of well-known songs of the Bible, see Appendix B.)

2

Songs of Moses

Music washes away from the soul the dust of everyday life.
—Berthold Auerbach

TO IMAGINE what music might have sounded like in ancient times is a wonderful exercise. How different it must have been from music of today. Instruments of antiquity, so relatively rare in our times, such as the lyre, harp, lute, and horns literally fashioned from animal horns, produced sounds we might hear only on eclectic folk recordings or special programming from National Public Radio. The gap between what we know as fact and what must be left to speculation when studying all the music of the Bible is wide, indeed. Not only do the possible rhythms and sounds themselves stretch the imagination, one of the most significant figures of the Old Testament stretches the imagination in another way.

Moses, not one whom we often think of as an inspired musician, is in fact the author of numerous songs that captured for his people's memory the mighty acts of God. Moses. A musician? Surprisingly, yes. The only man in the Bible to be adopted by a princess, to be buried by the Lord, and most importantly, to see God face to face, Moses must have heard a cacophony of sounds, and these sounds were intertwined in three forty-year periods of his life.

Moses lived from 1525 to 1405 B.C. and spent forty years each in Egypt, Midian, and the wilderness around Canaan, where he died in the land of Moab. In the first forty years of his life, Moses learned to be somebody. As the prince of Egypt, the adopted son of Pharaoh's daughter, he sang the songs of Egypt's glory and Israel's bondage.

During his second forty years, he learned what it was to be nobody. After killing an Egyptian who had beaten a Hebrew, Moses fled across the Red Sea to Midian. While there, he married and returned to Egypt with a new song, "Let my people go" (Exod. 5:1 NIV).

In the third forty-year period, Moses learned that God had a plan for everybody. God liberated his chosen people and established them in the Promised Land.

Moses wrote the first five books of the Old Testament, a vast amount of material that comprises the Books of the Law or the Pentateuch. Only three out of possibly numerous songs he may have written are preserved in the Scriptures:

- The Red Sea Song (Exod. 15:1–18)

- Moses' Psalm (Ps. 90)

- A Farewell Song (Deut. 32:1–43)

Let us examine each of these songs more closely.

The Red Sea Song

Sing to the LORD for he is highly exalted. —Exodus 15:1 (NIV)

God's plan to free the Israelites from slavery in Egypt and give them a home in Canaan began by liberating them from Egypt's pursuing army of chariots and horsemen at the Red Sea. Trapped at the edge of the Red Sea with nowhere to run, the Israelites witnessed God's power when the waters of the sea parted. As the Israelites made their way across the path of dry ground opening before them, they witnessed God's mighty hand as he crushed Pharaoh's army beneath the swirling waters.

Moses and his sister, Miriam, joined the throng of men, women and children as they watched their deliverance from slavery and imminent death. On cue, almost is if they had been cast in a Broadway musical, the crowd burst into song. This song, called the Red Sea Song, set to music the first poem of the freed nation, a celebration that was, most likely, more fantastic than even Cecil B. DeMille could have orchestrated.

Miriam was a ninety-three year old woman when she sang this song. As Moses' older sister, she had watched over him in his watertight bassinet by the edge of the Nile. When Pharaoh's daughter came to the river to bathe, saw the beautiful baby Moses floating among the rushes, and decided to adopt him, it was the courageous young Miriam who approached the princess. As Miriam drew near to the royal daughter, she offered to find a nurse for him, and of course, as we well know, brought Moses' mother to be his nurse.

In a desert land, as in the Scriptures themselves, water is often a source of spiritual significance as well as physical sustenance. At the Red Sea, Miriam participated in her people's salvation as the waters parted, sparing the lives of the Israelites and crashing back in on the Egyptian army. When the waters of the Red Sea opened, offering a miraculous path to liberation, proclaiming the power and faithfulness of God came as naturally to Moses and Miriam as taking their next breath or putting one foot in front of the other. The most ancient composition of its kind still in existence, this divinely inspired song was initially used by Moses and Miriam to instruct Israel in expressing praise and gratitude to the Lord.

Three Tambourines and a Drum from Ancient Egypt[1]
Figure 2.1

Exodus tells us Moses and the Israelites sang this song as an offering to the Lord and "Then Miriam the prophetess, the sister of Aaron, took the timbrel in her hand; and all the women went out after her with timbrels and with dances" (Exod. 15:20 NKJV). Miriam had the honor of singing the final verse of the song of praise to the triumphant congregation. Her song was exuberant, full of zeal for all that the Lord had done. God was her strength, and she led the excited throng in celebrating God's deliverance of their nation. As they celebrated, Moses and Miriam led the victorious crowd of 600,000 men and all the women and children with them in praise of the God of power and might.

Well over 2,000,000 voices of men, women, and children soared up to heaven that day, each voice filled with gratitude and praise. As our own songs of deliverance often carry pleas and cries for help to leave painful circumstances, let us rest in the reassurance offered by the Red Sea Song: that God is divine and wants the best for us, that when we, too, experience redemption, we will again find ourselves lifting our voices in praise. Let us sing to the Lord!

Sung by All:
I will sing to the LORD,
For He has triumphed gloriously!
The horse and its rider He has thrown into the sea!

Sung by Men:
The LORD is my strength and song,
And He has become my salvation;
He is my God, and I will praise Him;
My father's God, and I will exalt Him.
The LORD is a man of war;
The LORD is His name.

Sung by Miriam and the Women with Tambourines:
Sing to the LORD,
For he has triumphed gloriously!
The horse and its rider
He has thrown into the sea.

Sung by All:
Pharaoh's chariots and his army
He has cast into the sea;

His chosen captains also are drowned in the Red Sea.
The depths have covered them;
They sank to the bottom like a stone.
Your right hand, O LORD, has become glorious in power;
Your right hand, O LORD, has dashed the enemy in pieces.
And in the greatness of Your excellence
You have overthrown those who rose against You;
You sent forth Your wrath; it consumed them like stubble.
And with the blast of Your nostrils
The waters were gathered together;
The floods stood upright like a heap;
The depths congealed in the heart of the sea.

Sung by Miriam and the Women with Tambourines:
Sing to the LORD,
For he has triumphed gloriously!
The horse and its rider
He has thrown into the sea.

Sung by All:
The enemy said, "I will pursue, I will overtake,
I will divide the spoil;
My desire shall be satisfied on them.
I will draw my sword,
My hand shall destroy them."
You blew with Your wind,
The sea covered them;
They sank like lead in the mighty waters.
Who is like You, O LORD, among the gods?
Who is like You, glorious in holiness,
Fearful in praises, doing wonders?
You stretched out Your right hand;
The earth swallowed them.
You in Your mercy have led forth
The people whom You have redeemed;
You have guided them in your strength
To Your holy habitation.

Sung by Miriam and the Women with Tambourines:
Sing to the LORD,
For he has triumphed gloriously!
The horse and its rider
He has thrown into the sea.

Sung by All:
The people will hear and be afraid;
Sorrow will take hold of the inhabitants of Philistia.
Then the chiefs of Edom will be dismayed;
The mighty men of Moab,
Trembling will take hold of them;
All the inhabitants of Canaan will melt away.
Fear and dread will fall on them;
By the greatness of Your arm
They will be as still as a stone,
Till Your people pass over, O LORD,
Till the people pass over
Whom you have purchased.
You will bring them in and plant them
In the mountain of Your inheritance,
In the place, O LORD, which You have made
For Your own dwelling,
The Sanctuary, O LORD, which your hands have established.

Grand Chorus Sung by All:
The LORD shall reign forever and ever.
(Exod. 15:1–18 NKJV)

Crossing the Red Sea was only the beginning of the Israelite's adventure that would last the next forty years. Three months after leaving Egypt they arrived at Mount Sinai, where Yahweh confirmed His covenant with them when he spoke to Moses.

"Now therefore, if you will indeed obey My voice and keep My covenant, then you shall be a special treasure to Me above all people; for all the earth is Mine. And you shall be to Me a kingdom of priests and a holy nation." These are the words which you shall speak to the children of Israel. (Exod. 19:5–6 NKJV)

Moses did deliver the commandment to the people, and with the crescendo of the Red Sea rescue still resounding in their minds and memories, the people of Israel readily agreed to do what God had asked of them. Before their journey continued, one more mighty act of God concluded their time at Sinai: the giving of the Ten Commandments to Moses. What more vivid, direct, and unequivocal confirmation of Moses' leadership could the Israelites have witnessed?

But human nature is fickle, and our memory of God's faithfulness is often short-lived. Boredom with manna, lack of water, and long days and nights in the wilderness led to incessant complaining, discord, and strain. During this time of wandering, a number of events occurred while the Israelites tried and failed again and again to be faithful to God's will, including a war with Canaan, the death of Miriam, and God's punishment of Moses and Aaron, a punishment that came as a direct result of Moses' disobeying Yahweh's specific instructions concerning the water shortage. Instead of speaking to a certain rock to produce water as God directed, Moses struck the rock. Though water gushed from the rock (Num. 20:11), and the rebellious crowd drank their fill, the defiant act of Moses striking the rock in anger resulted in God's decree that Moses and Aaron would not lead their assembly into the Promised Land.

> Then the LORD spoke to Moses and Aaron, "Because you did not believe Me, to hallow Me in the eyes of the children of Israel, therefore you shall not bring this assembly into the land which I have given them." (Num. 20:12 NKJV)

What followed was a scene of fiery serpents sent by God when the Israelites continued to speak out against the years of wandering through the wilderness.

> "Why have you brought us up out of Egypt to die in the wilderness? For there is no food and no water, and our soul loathes this worthless bread!" (Num. 21:5 NKJV)

Even after deliverance from the poisonous fangs, they continued to cry out for water. After still more wandering, Moses led the nation of Israel to the northern border of Moab, where the book of Numbers recounts another turning point marked by music. Once again, despite their speaking out against God, their discouragement, and frequent questioning of God, Yahweh provided for their well-being. Once again, God was faithful by leading them to a plentiful source of water.

> From there [the border of Moab] they continued to Beer; that is the well of which the LORD said to Moses, "Gather the people together, and I will give them water." (Num. 21:16 NRSV)

After a journey through a hot and dry land, cold water from a well would lift anyone's spirit. The children of Israel broke out in musical praise, known as the Song of the Well, to express their joy and gratitude for the faithfulness of Yahweh. Then Israel sang this song:

> Spring up, O well!—Sing to it!—
> the well that the leaders sank,
> that the nobles of the people dug,
> with the scepter, with the staff.
> (Num. 21:17–18 NRSV)

The book of the Wars of the Lord (a book mentioned in the Bible, but no longer extant) may be a collection of songs written to preserve traditions of the twelve tribes and to glorify Yahweh for protecting His people in the wilderness. Alternately, Moses may have read about the well in the small desert town of Beer in a previously existing version of the Wars of the Lord. Either way, at a place called Beer in the region of the wadis of the River Arnon, Yahweh told Moses to assemble the people so water could be provided and the God's covenant once again be made manifest.

Perhaps the water flowed near to the surface of the ground, and under Moses' direction, the leaders of the tribes dug through the dry earth so fresh water could spring forth. Perhaps the discovery of water came another way. No matter what actually happened that day at Beer, what we do know was the people of God responded by singing to the sight of life-saving water. And once again, words of praise were insufficient for the depth of emotion; music turned words of praise and elation into an experience of corporate worship. Music and song transcended the words themselves. Despite the grumbling of twelve wandering tribes, God still called this moody, complaining, rebellious mob His chosen people. Amazing grace begins early in the story of the people of God.

Moses' Psalm

The third song of Moses is the oldest known psalm ever recorded. Moses wrote it at the close of his forty years of leading his people through the wilderness. The imagery in this psalm is borrowed from the desert experience of long years of wandering in a harsh and barren land, images which include:

- The desert streams, which soon dry up
- The night watch in the camp
- The short-lived growth of grass before the fragile blades are blasted by desert winds

This psalm is full of melancholy and reflects the spirit of the Israelites as they conducted daily funerals and wandered aimlessly in the desert heat. Moses beautifully illustrates their life together throughout his song. The evidence found in the similarity of the phrasing, word choice, and expression to that found in the Pentateuch supports the conclusion of Mosaic authorship, though some scholars have questioned its origin.

In Ps. 90, Moses contrasts the eternity of God with the transience of human life (Ps. 90:1–6). He goes on to link the brevity and troublesomeness of human existence with God's displeasure of sin (Ps. 90:7–12). Moses ends his song with a prayer for God's forgiveness and favor (Ps. 90:13–17).

These texts have been used for centuries as part of burial services. Like other odes in the Psalter, this Psalm has had wide historic influence. For example, Charles V of England, the champion of the pope and enemy of Martin Luther, became one of the Reformers in his love for the psalms. In September 1558, as Charles lay on his deathbed, he requested passages be read from his favorite psalm, Ps. 90. At his request, he received the sacrament, but added, "It may not be necessary; yet it [the psalm] is good company on so long a journey."

Lord, You have been our dwelling place in all generations.

Before the mountains were born
Or You gave birth to the earth and the world,
Even from everlasting to everlasting,
You are God.

You turn man back into dust
And say, "Return, O children of men."

For a thousand years in Your sight
Are like yesterday when it passes by,
Or [as] a watch in the night.

You have swept them away like a flood, they fall asleep;
In the morning they are like grass which sprouts anew.

In the morning it flourishes and sprouts anew;
Toward evening it fades and withers away.

For we have been consumed by Your anger
And by Your wrath we have been dismayed.

You have placed our iniquities before You,
Our secret [sins] in the light of Your presence.

For all our days have declined in Your fury;
We have finished our years like a sigh.

As for the days of our life, they contain seventy years,
Or if due to strength, eighty years,
Yet their pride is [but] labor and sorrow;
For soon it is gone and we fly away.

Who understands the power of Your anger
And Your fury, according to the fear that is due You?

So teach us to number our days,
That we may present to You a heart of wisdom.

Do return, O LORD; how long [will it be?] And be sorry for Your
   servants.

O satisfy us in the morning with Your lovingkindness,
That we may sing for joy and be glad all our days.

Make us glad according to the days You have afflicted us,
[And] the years we have seen evil.

Let Your work appear to Your servants
And Your majesty to their children.

Let the favor of the Lord our God be upon us;
And confirm for us the work of our hands;
Yes, confirm the work of our hands.
(Ps. 90:1–17 NASB)

A Farewell Song

Moses recites his third song as a solo in front of the assembly of Israel. He introduces his prophetic and historic song by expressing his
desire to effectively communicate his words, a prayer that ministers
across the world as preachers take the pulpit each Sunday.

Give ear, O heavens, and I will speak;
let the earth hear the words of my mouth.

May my teaching drop like the rain,
my speech condense like the dew;
like gentle rain on grass,
like showers on new growth.

For I will proclaim the name of the LORD;
ascribe greatness to our God!
(Deut. 32:1–3 NRSV)

Contrasting the character of God (32:4) with the corruption of the
people (32:5–6), Moses calls the Israelites to remember God's kindness
(32:7).

The Rock, his work is perfect,
and all his ways are just.
A faithful God, without deceit,
just and upright is he;

yet his degenerate children have dealt falsely with him,
a perverse and crooked generation.

Do you thus repay the LORD,
O foolish and senseless people?
Is not he your father, who created you,
who made you and established you?

Remember the days of old,
Consider the years long past;
ask your father, and he will inform you;
your elders, and they will tell you.
(Deut. 32:4–7 NRSV)

He continues by recounting God's interactions with them during their wilderness trek (32:8–14), their ingratitude and iniquity (32:15–18) and finally, the threat of God's judgment (32:19–28).

When the Most High apportioned the nations,
when he divided humankind,
he fixed the boundaries of the peoples
according to the number of the gods;

the LORD's own portion was his people, Jacob his allotted share.

He sustained him in a desert land,
in a howling wilderness waste;
he shielded him, cared for him, guarded him as the apple of his eye.

As an eagle stirs up its nest, and hovers over its young;
as it spreads its wings, takes them up, and bears them aloft on its
    pinions,

the LORD alone guided him; no foreign god was with him.

He set him atop the heights of the land,
and fed him with produce of the field;

he nursed him with honey from the crags, with oil from flinty
    rock;

curds from the herd, and milk from the flock, with fat of lambs
    and rams; Bashan bulls and goats, together with the choicest
    wheat—
you drank fine wine from the blood of grapes.

Jacob ate his fill; Jeshurun grew fat, and kicked.
You grew fat, bloated, and gorged!
He abandoned God who made him,
and scoffed at the Rock of his salvation.

They made him jealous with strange gods,
with abhorrent things they provoked him.

They sacrificed to demons, not God,
to deities they had never known,
to new ones recently arrived,
whom your ancestors had not feared.

You were unmindful of the Rock that bore you;
you forgot the God who gave you birth.

The LORD saw [this], and was jealous;
he spurned his sons and daughters.

He said: I will hide my face from them, I will see what their end
    will be; for they are a perverse generation, children in whom
    there is no faithfulness.

They made me jealous with what is no god,
provoked me with their idols.
So I will make them jealous with what is no people,
provoke them with a foolish nation.

For a fire is kindled by my anger,
and burns to the depths of Sheol;
it devours the earth and its increase,
and sets on fire the foundations of the mountains.

I will heap disasters upon them,
spend my arrows against them:

wasting hunger, burning consumption, bitter pestilence.
The teeth of beasts I will send against them,
with venom of things crawling in the dust.

In the street the sword shall bereave,
and in chambers terror, for young man and woman alike,
nursing child and old gray head.

I thought to scatter them and blot out the memory of them
    from humankind;

but I feared provocation by the enemy,
for their adversaries might misunderstand
and say, "Our hand is triumphant;
it was not the LORD who did all this."

They are a nation void of sense;
there is no understanding in them.
(Deut. 32:4–28 NRSV)

Moses nears the end of his song by painting a picture of God's lamentation over their sins and God's act of grace on their behalf, as well as reproaches for their acceptance of idolatry.

If they were wise, they would understand this;
they would discern what the end would be.

How could one have routed a thousand, and two put a myriad to
    flight, unless their Rock had sold them, the LORD had given
    them up?

Indeed their rock is not like our Rock; our enemies are fools.

Their vine comes from the vinestock of Sodom, from the
    vineyards of Gomorrah;

their grapes are grapes of poison, their clusters are bitter;
their wine is the poison of serpents, the cruel venom of asps.

Is not this laid up in store with me, sealed up in my treasuries?

Vengeance is mine, and recompense, for time when their foot
  shall slip; because the day of their calamity is at hand, their
  doom comes swiftly.

Indeed the LORD will vindicate his people, have compassion on
  his servants, when he sees that their power is gone, neither
  bond nor free remaining.

Then he will say: Where are their gods,
the rock in which they took refuge,

who ate the fat of their sacrifices, and drank the wine of their
  libations?
Let them rise up and help you, let them be your protection!

See now that I, even I, am he; there is no god beside me.
I kill and I make alive; I wound and I heal; and no one can
  deliver from my hand.

For I lift up my hand to heaven, and swear: As I live forever,

when I whet my flashing sword, and my hand takes hold on
  judgment; I will take vengeance on my adversaries, and will
  repay those who hate me.

I will make my arrows drunk with blood, and my sword shall
  devour flesh—with the blood of the slain and the captives,
  from the long-haired enemy.
(Deut. 32:29–42 NRSV)

Moses concludes his solo with God's promise of salvation to the
Gentiles.

Praise, O heavens, his people,
worship him, all you gods!
For he will avenge the blood of his children,
and take vengeance on his adversaries;
he will repay those who hate him, and cleanse the land for his
  people.
(Deut. 32:43 NRSV)

With Joshua, son of Nun, Moses sings the words of this song in the presence of the nation of Israel. When they've finished, Moses cautions the crowd, "Take to heart all the words that I am giving in witness against you today; give them as a command to your children, so that they may diligently observe all the words of this law. This is no trifling matter for you, but rather your very life; through it you may live long in the land that you are crossing over the Jordan to possess" (Deut. 32:46–47 NRSV).

May we also take to heart the words given to Moses by God on that day at the foot of Mount Nebo. Indeed, the Word of the Lord is no trifling matter for us, but rather our very life. May we, too, always remember that our God is a just God who saves through grace; that He alone is worthy to be praised. Moses is, most certainly, an example for us: An example of how to respond to adversity, to times of wandering and uncertainty, and ultimately to God's grace and redemption. Moses sang a song of farewell before ascending Mount Nebo, the place from which he would view the Promise Land, knowing that he would not be the one to lead his people triumphantly into the land of milk and honey.

> On Jordan's stormy banks I stand,
> And cast a wishful eye
> To Canaan's fair and happy land,
> Where my possessions lie.[2]

Yet he sang a song of proclaiming the faithfulness of God, the justice of God's judgments, the lamentation of a righteous God over our sin, and finally, God's promise of salvation. Our songs today have the same notes as the songs of Moses—God is our salvation, our strength, and our song. Let us raise our voices in faithful praise as we journey through our own desert plains and mountaintops. As saved ones, let us sing!

3

Songs of Deborah and Hannah

The rhythms of our lives comprise the symphony of God's creation—a work which has been in progress longer than any other. —Peggy Moon

MUSIC IS FORMATIVE, of that there is no doubt. "To sing is to be formed into what one sings," writes Wendy Wright in an article titled, "Sing to the Lord a New Song."[1] Thus, is it not in keeping with the Lord's covenant that even the recorded history of a chosen people be preserved in such a manner that the Word is both memorable *and* formative? Open your Bible to Ps. 100 and sprinkled across the page like musical notes on a staff are the verbs "sing," "praise," and "give thanks." "Make a joyful noise to the LORD," we are told again and again. "Come into His presence with singing" (Ps. 100:1, 2 RSV).

This covenant relationship given to us by Yahweh at the time of Abraham, affirmed repeatedly through the lives of Old Testament heroes such as those we've been studying, and forever sealed in the Risen Christ, is a relationship in which music of prayer and praise is as necessary and natural as breathing.

"O sing to the LORD a new song!" (Ps. 98:1 RSV) Indeed, the very telling of the stories of the Old Testament by the reciting of poems, psalms, and hymns informs our understanding of the character of God in much the same way the Word of the Lord formed the twelve tribes of Israel. To try to imagine the pathos in the sounds of lament, the anguish of a people crying out for deliverance, one needs only to look back to the enduring spirituals born of slavery on American shores. "Whatever people can say with passion and in heightened speech they will end up singing in some form," writes Don E. Saliers.[2]

From the restless, wandering tribes to a faithful Kingdom united during the reigns of Saul, David, and Solomon—such is the power of God to transform those who seek His Holiness. Yet, before we move into the rich, lyrical treasure of the Psalms, the songbook of the Hebrews, and into the prophetic poetry of Isaiah, this study of the ancient songs of Israel would be incomplete without first looking at the vibrant songs of two influential women of the Old Testament: Deborah, a judge (Judg. 4:4), and Hannah, a barren, but favored wife.

The Song of Deborah and Barak

Awake, awake, Deborah! Awake, awake, utter a song! Arise, Barak, lead away your captives. —Judges 5:12 (NRSV)

Of all the ancient music we've reviewed, the victorious song of Deborah and Barak is one of the most eloquent and expressive pieces of poetry ever written. Music is a reflection of the context and culture in which it is created, as is all art, and there is no better example of this fact than the Old Testament story of an unusual judge, a military leader, and a formidable foe.

Because this story in the Old Testament is perhaps a little less familiar than the story of Moses, it is wise for us to look at the historical context of this ancient song, a literary masterpiece of "vivid descriptions, striking imagery, effective repetitions, and skillful use of various poetic techniques."[3]

The Scriptures have taken us from the beginning of creation through the call of Abraham, to the miracle of the Exodus and the wilderness journey, all events told and retold among the Israelites as part of their, and our, salvation history. The next major historical period in the life of this rag-tag, wandering company of loosely formed tribes is often called the "Settlement of the Land."

With the death of Moses and the succession of leadership passed to Joshua, the Israelites enter the Promised Land and begin to build their lives. May we not be misled into believing this was an orderly, peaceful process, however. Bearing in mind that these were tribal people, accustomed to surviving in the wilderness, we can safely assume that this was a willful lot indeed—headstrong and full of zeal to conquer this long awaited land. In order to maintain some order and establish civil law, judges were appointed to serve the tribal regions, and though their specific duties are not fully known, we do know that some presided over civil disputes and legal matters while others were primarily military leaders.

One judge, however, stands apart from the others in this period of conquest and settlement. Not only is Deborah the only woman among the twelve leaders presented in the book of Judges, Deborah stands apart by the very nature of the tasks she performed. Deborah served as both legal counsel *and* military strategist, a distinction that sets her apart. But the third distinctive aspect tells us unequivocally that the Lord God had His hand on her, for she was a prophetess. Though identified as "wife of Lappidoth" in most English translations, there is no other mention of Lappidoth in the Holy Scriptures, and we know of no Lappidoth in Hebrew history. However, we do know the meaning of *lappidoth* in Hebrew can be "torches," and the literal translation of Deborah is "bee." It's quite possible that the Hebrew phrase rendered "wife of Lappidoth," is perhaps identifying Deborah as a "fiery" or "spirited" woman as noted in the New English Bible.

After leading the Hebrews out of bondage by a courageous man named Moses, God once again provides courageous leadership at a critical juncture in the life of the Hebrews. This time, however, the one whom God called was not a man with the brawny strength needed to carry heavy clay tablets down a rugged mountain. No, this time the call to leadership was given to a wise, "spirited" prophetess named Deborah who knew just the right military leader to summon for the task at hand!

The writer of Judges is making it clear that this was both a military *and* a spiritual battle, for the Israelites had again done "what was evil in the sight of the LORD." After twenty years of oppression they "cried out to the LORD for help" (Judg. 4:1, 3 NRSV) and God who is faithful and just heeded their pleas.

As Deborah watched the advancing enemy army led by the Canaanite commander Sisera and summoned the commander Barak to lead the Galilean tribes against the attacking foes, they both knew this was a fight for the land and the souls of the Hebrew people. Further evidence of the importance this story holds in the sacred text is the very fact that the story of Deborah and Barak is preserved in both prose *and* poetry.

Deborah orders Barak: get ready; call out the army, all ten thousand men; we are under attack by the Canaanite commander Sisera. But Barak, knowing of Deborah's reputation for wisdom and spiritual insight, refuses to lead the tribes into battle against the superior army of Sisera unless Deborah comes with him.

> "If you will go with me, I will go; but if you will not go with me, I will not go." And she said, "I will surely go with you; nevertheless, the road on which you are going will not lead to your glory, for the LORD will sell Sisera into the hand of a woman." (Judg. 4:8–9 NRSV)

The stage is set; the godless enemy has greater might and the military advantage of iron chariots (Judg. 4:3). Judges 5:6–23 recounts the myriad of battles that ensued along the way from Canaan. As Sisera approached the land of Israel with nine hundred iron chariots bearing down on the Israelites, a miracle occurred. The skies opened up and rain poured down. Here we move from the prose telling to the poetic rendering:

> LORD, when you went out from Seir,
> when you marched from the region of Edom,
> the earth trembled,
> and the heavens poured,
> the clouds indeed poured water.

> The mountains quaked before the LORD, the One of Sinai,
> before the LORD, the God of Israel.
> (Judg. 5:4–5 NRSV)

As the Canaanite warriors, horses, and chariots found themselves mired in mud and rushing waters, the Israelites won the battle in a resounding victory. But the enemy commander, Sisera, escaped on foot, fleeing to the tent of Jael, the wife of Heber, "for there was peace between [them]" (4:17 NRSV). There, Jael, an Israelite, killed the exhausted Sisera as he slept, thus fulfilling Deborah's prophecy to Barak that "the LORD will sell Sisera into the hand of a woman" (4:9 NRSV).

Most blessed among women is Jael
The wife of Heber the Kenite;
Blessed is she among women in tents.

He asked for water, she gave milk;
She brought out cream
in a lordly bowl.

She stretched her hand to the tent peg,
Her right hand to the workmen's hammer;
She pounded Sisera,
She pierced his head,
She split and struck through his temple.

At her feet he sank, he fell, he lay still;
At her feet he sank, he fell;
Where he sank, there he fell dead.
(Judg. 5:24–27 NKJV)

The immensity of the problem facing the Israelites, and the miraculous intervention of God, were just cause for Deborah and Barak to praise God for their deliverance. Valiant though they were, the judge and her military leader realized the majesty and might of God, and following this victory, their response could only be one of thankfulness and praise.

Though Scriptures tell us that Deborah and Barak both "sang on that day" (5:1 NKJV), the Hebrew verb in 5:1 is the feminine singular, meaning Deborah is the singer. In verse 12 (NRSV), Deborah is the one called to sing: "Awake, awake, Deborah! Awake, awake, utter a song!" Deborah knew how to say "thank you" for the mystery and miracle of God's faithfulness.

The Song of Deborah, history in poetic form, mirrors the pattern of the 410–year period between the death of Joshua and Samuel's anointing of a king. The song begins with praise of God and the heroes through whom God brings deliverance (5:1–12), moves into the description of the battle, a time of turmoil and strife (13–23), and concludes with the defeat of their enemies and a period of "rest" or deliverance from oppression.

Music and the lyrical repetition found in singing "is one very powerful way in which we become re-made in the image of God,"[4] a truth
long understood and practiced by the Israelites. The great hymns of the
Christian church do the same for us as the songs of ancient Israel did
thousands of years ago for the fledgling nation of God. Music brings to
mind our common memories, teaches us of God's faithfulness, and
holds before us that to which we are called. As Deborah concluded her
praise to God, she finished her song with a prayer seeking God's judgment on His enemies and His blessing on His followers, though we
must remember that in Christ, the new covenant, we are commanded
to love our enemies and pray for them.

> So perish all your enemies, O LORD! But may your friends be like
> the sun as it rises in its might. (Judg. 5:31 NRSV)

Hannah's Prophetic Hymn

*Hannah prayed and said . . . "There is no Holy One like the LORD, no one be-
sides you; there is no Rock like our God." —1 Samuel 2:1, 2 (NRSV)*
Another woman who knew how to say "thank you" was Hannah,
the childless but favored wife of Elkanah. A godly, humble woman who
gave birth to Samuel, Hannah withstood years of derision, ridicule,
and provocation from her rival, Peninnah, who was Elkanah's second
wife and the mother of his heirs. This poignant story of a woman griev-
ing her childless state, told in the first chapter of 1 Samuel, is a story
again that has historical and spiritual meaning of much greater significance than the telling of one simple woman's longing for a child and
her plea for the LORD God to "look on the misery of your servant, and
remember me" (1 Sam. 1:11 NRSV).

Only the birth of Jesus rivals the detail and importance given to the
birth narrative of Samuel, and of the four writers of the Gospels, only
Luke tells us "the rest of the story," as the well-known commentator
Paul Harvey would say. Matthew reduces the story of Jesus' birth to a
cursory eight verses; Mark jumps from the baptism of John to the baptism of Jesus, skipping over any details of his birth at all. John, whose
Gospel is richly laden with powerful, compelling imagery, moves im-

mediately to the central theme of his Gospel: the "divine Savior" has come into the world, was rejected by many, and gives eternal life to those who believe. Unlike many heroes of the Bible about whom we hear only after they come into a position of leadership, "the story of Samuel, like those of Moses and Samson, begins before his birth."[5]

So as we study the Song of Hannah, let us first ask why Hannah's story is told with such length, poignancy, and vividness. Indeed, before this barren woman sings her song of thanksgiving in Chapter 2, she is accused of drunkenness and behavior unfitting for the house of the Lord in the first chapter of 1 Samuel!

> Hannah rose and presented herself before the LORD. Now Eli the priest was sitting on the seat beside the doorpost of the temple of the LORD. She was deeply distressed and prayed to the LORD, and wept bitterly.

> As she continued praying before the LORD, Eli observed her mouth. Hannah was praying silently; only her lips moved, but her voice was not heard; therefore Eli thought she was drunk. So Eli said to her, "How long will you make a drunken spectacle of yourself? Put away your wine." But Hannah answered, "No, my lord, I am a woman deeply troubled; I have drunk neither wine nor strong drink, but I have been pouring out my soul before the LORD. Do not regard your servant as a worthless woman, for I have been speaking out of my great anxiety and vexation all this time." Then Eli answered, "Go in peace; the God of Israel grant the petition you have made to Him." (1 Sam. 1:9–10, 12–17 NRSV)

Hannah was a devoted woman of great piety, of this we are assured. Just as Luke tells the story of Mary and Joseph, 1 Samuel tells of the events leading up to the birth of Samuel from the woman's perspective, something a bit unusual in the Old Testament, something that again tells us this story bears great importance to the ancient people of Israel, and therefore, to us as well.

As we noted at the beginning of this study of all the music in the Bible, the songs, stories, and prayers told in Scripture all point to major theological themes. Deliverance, the reversal of human fortunes, lifting up the lowly and bringing down the mighty, the intervention of God in human history—these are but a few of the major themes running through the Scriptures. The Song of Hannah is "prophetic" because of the clear presentation of these themes. Hannah was a barren woman, a woman with no future. Without a leader anointed by Yahweh's blessing, the tribes of Israel were a people without a future, fragmented and forgetful of the importance of following God's ways. As Walter Brueggemann says, "This is no ordinary narrative. . . . The story invites us with Israel to reflect on the question, How is a new future possible amid the barrenness that renders us bitter, hopeless, and fruitless?"[6] Hannah's song is an exuberant, resounding affirmation that with God, all things are possible, for indeed, "there is none holy as the LORD" (1 Sam. 2:2 KJV)!

> My heart rejoiceth in the LORD,
> mine horn is exalted in the LORD:
> my mouth is enlarged over mine enemies;
> because I rejoice in thy salvation.
>
> There is none holy as the LORD:
> for there is none beside thee:
> neither is there any rock like our God.
>
> Talk no more so exceeding proudly;
> let not arrogancy come out of your mouth:
> for the LORD is a God of knowledge,
> and by him actions are weighed.
>
> The bows of the mighty men are broken,
> and they that stumbled are girded with strength.
>
> They that were full have hired out themselves for bread;
> and they that were hungry ceased:
> so that the barren hath born seven;
> and she that hath many children is waxed feeble.
>
> The LORD killeth, and maketh alive:
> he bringeth down to the grave, and bringeth up.
>
> The LORD maketh poor, and maketh rich: he bringeth low, and
> lifteth up.

He raiseth up the poor out of the dust,
and lifteth up the beggar from the dunghill,
to set them among princes,
and to make them inherit the throne of glory:
for the pillars of the earth are the LORD'S,
and he hath set the world upon them.

He will keep the feet of his saints,
and the wicked shall be silent in darkness;
for by strength shall no man prevail.

The adversaries of the LORD shall be broken to pieces;
out of heaven shall he thunder upon them:
the LORD shall judge the ends of the earth;
and he shall give strength unto his king,
and exalt the horn of his anointed.
(1 Sam. 2:1–10 KJV)

Let us conclude this study of the Song of Hannah with the fitting words of Walter Brueggemann: "Those overly fixed in their despair now have their life made over by the power of Yahweh."[7] Indeed, as do we!

4

Festival Songs of Zion

Oh, give thanks to the LORD!
Call upon His name;
Make known His deeds among the peoples!
Sing to Him, sing psalms to Him;
Talk of all His wondrous works! —1 Chronicles 16:8–9 (NKJV)

ALONG WITH DAILY WORSHIP, the law as set forth in the Pentateuch pre-scribed special festivals and feasts to be observed by the congregation. Held weekly, monthly, and yearly, the feasts and festivals were fixed by divine appointment for fellowship and worship. These were joyful times of song and celebration and served to preserve the memory of past mercies, depict God's holiness, and bring relief to the poor and oppressed. These special observances united Israel in a holy union and separated the twelve tribes from surrounding unbelieving nations. These special occasions expressed in song, ritual, and sacrifice the blessings and hopes of God's gathered people.

Moreover, the law established each seventh year as a Sabbatical Year, a year in which Israelite slaves were freed (Exod. 21:2–6; Deut. 15:12–18), land was to lie fallow (Exod. 23:10–11; Lev. 25:1–7), and debts were for-given (Deut. 15:1–6). The institution of this observance was intended to secure rest for the soil, to teach economy and foresight, and to impress upon the people their dependence on God (Lev. 25:20–21).

Every fiftieth year was designated as a Year of Jubilee (Lev. 25:8–55), a year in which the same practices were observed as the Sabbatical years with the additional requirement that land was returned to its original owner. One Hebrew name for "festival" *(hag)* derives from the verb "to dance" *(ḥagag),* implying that festivals were occasions of delight, deep joy, and music.

The Weekly Sabbath

Exod. 20:8–11

The weekly festival was the Sabbath, a day consecrated to rest and devotion (Exod. 20:8–11). On this day, those who lived near the temple attended the Sabbath observance and presented additional sacrifices (Lev. 24:8; Num. 28:9). Children received special *torah,* or instruction in God's laws, by studying and reciting the stories of their people. As the nation developed, people visited prophets on the Sabbath (2 Kgs. 4:23), and after the captivity, synagogues were erected throughout Palestine to provide weekly gatherings places for reading the sacred texts, worship and expounding upon "the reading from the Law and the Prophets" (Acts 13:15 NIV).

The Monthly New Moon

Num. 28:11–15

This monthly festival was held on the day of the new moon and was announced by the sound of silver trumpets (Num. 10:10). Labor was not prohibited, but rest was clearly the preferred (Amos 8:5), and additional sacrifices were offered (Num. 28:11–15). Numerous references to the observance of the new moon feast are made in the story of David and Jonathan (1 Sam. 20:5, 18, 24, 27). The new moon of the seventh month (Tishrei, or October; see fig. 4.1) commenced the civil New Year and was the most important of the new moon festivals.

The Yearly Pilgrimage Feasts

The great annual festivals prescribed by the law were all intended to be seasons of joyous thanksgiving and were commemorative of the kindness and favor of God. Three of the primary celebrations, also called pilgrimage festivals, required all the adult males in Israel to appear at the sanctuary (Exod. 23:14–17). These three pilgrimage feasts were the Passover and Feast of Unleavened Bread, the Feast of Weeks, and the Feast of Booths (Exod. 34:21–24).

The Passover and the Feast of Unleavened Bread

Exod. 12:1–28; 23:10–15

Passover kept alive the memory of the destruction of the Egyptians' firstborn, the sparing of the Israelites, and their departure from Egypt. It began on the eve of the fourteenth of Nisan (see fig. 4.1) and was reckoned from the fifteenth to the twenty-first. Each family removed all leaven from the house, and the paschal lamb (a yearling ram or goat, Exod. 12:3–5) was slain before the altar (Deut. 16:5–6). At the Passover meal, the master of the family broke unleavened bread and distributed it to each, not fewer than ten nor more than twenty being admitted to the feast. After the third cup, the "cup of blessing," was drunk, the family sang praises together. In later times, these praises came from Pss. 115–118 and sometimes Pss. 120–137. During each subsequent day of the festival, additional sacrifices were offered, and on the sixteenth of Nisan, the first ears of corn were presented at the sanctuary. With this offering, the harvest commenced. It was at this feast and with the third cup that our Lord instituted the Last Supper (Matt. 26:17–30; Mark 14:12–26; 1 Cor. 10:16–18).

The Feast of Pentecost or the Feast of Weeks

Exod. 23:16; Lev. 23:15–22

Fifty days or seven weeks after Passover came the feast of Pentecost, also called the "Festival of Weeks" or the festival of harvest. It marked the beginning of the wheat harvest when loaves made of the new grain were offered as "first fruits" of the harvest (Lev. 23:17). Families presented burnt offerings at this time, as well, contributing to the well-being of the priests and the poor (Lev. 23:18–22, specifically v. 19). Jews residing outside of Palestine (those in the Diaspora) often chose this occasion for visiting Jerusalem (Acts 2:5).

Hebrew Calendar	Corresponding Modern Months	Farm Seasons
Nisan	March/April	Begin barley harvest
Iyyar	April/May	Barley harvest
Sivan	May/June	Wheat harvest
Tammuz	June/July	
Av	July/August	Grape, fig, olive ripe
Elul	August/September	Vintage begins
Tishrei	September/October	Early rains; plowing
Heshvan	October/November	Wheat, barley sowing
Kislev	November/December	
Tebeth	December/January	Rainy winter months
Shebat	January/February	New year for trees
Adar	February/March	Almonds blooming

Hebrew Calendar
Figure 4.1

The Feast of Booths

Num. 29:12–39; Lev. 23:33–36

"On the fifteenth day of the seventh month you shall have a holy convocation," Moses told the Hebrews (Num. 29:12 NRSV); "you shall not work at your occupations. Seven days you shall present the LORD's offerings by fire." (Lev. 23:35–36 NRSV) Thus began the Festival of Booths or the Feast of Tabernacles, the most joyous of the three pilgrimage festivals (Deut. 16:9–16). Also called the "Great Hosanna," this occasion celebrated and consecrated the ingathering of crops from the autumn harvest, and possibly more importantly, was a festival ordained to commemorate the sojourning of the Israelites in the wilderness.

During the Festival of Booths, observed in the autumn month of Tishrei (October), the people were commanded to construct booths out of palm tree branches and willows throughout the city "so that your generations may know that I made the people of Israel live in booths when I brought them out of the land of Egypt" (Lev. 23:4–43). More public sacrifices were offered than at any other celebration (Lev. 23:38–40; Num. 29:39). On the last day of the feast, water was drawn from the pool of Siloam, carried with great pomp to the temple, and poured before the altar (Isa. 12:3; John 7:37–38). Priests also ascended the steps that separated the court of the women from the inner court, singing the Psalms of Degrees (120–134), the same Songs of Ascents that the people had sung as they climbed up to Jerusalem for the autumn festivals.

Another Yearly Feast

The Feast of Trumpets

Lev. 23:23–25; Num. 29:1–6
The most important of the new moon festivals, this feast functioned as New Year's Day and was celebrated on the first day of the new moon of Tishrei (October). Called *Rosh Hashanah* (head or first of the year), it marked the start of the secular year with the blowing of trumpets (Lev. 23:23–25). Several different Hebrew words are translated "trumpets," which we will look at in greater detail when we review the musical instruments of the ancient Hebrews. The religious year, however, began with Nisan, the Passover month.

Ancient Jewish Festivals Still Observed

The Feast of Lights

John 10:22
Emerging from Hebrew victories that came well after feasts were appointed by Moses, the Feast of Lights, or *Ḥanukkah,* recalls the Maccabean revolt during a time of religious persecution of the Jews in which the Temple was desecrated (167 B.C.). Under the leadership of Judas Maccabee, Jerusalem was retaken, the Temple was restored and purified, and the Hebrews' faith and worship in Yahweh preserved. Celebrated for eight days starting on the twenty-fifth of Kislev (overlapping our

December), this festival is not mentioned in the Old Testament, but it bears striking similarities to Solomon's consecration of the Temple (I Kgs. 8:2). The celebration of this festival is referenced in John 10:22.

The Feast of Purim

Esther 9

Celebrated on March fourteenth and fifteenth, *Purim* is a minor holiday in the Jewish calendar commemorating the heroism of Esther. Queen Esther's actions at a critical time prevented the execution of the Jews, a plan conceived by Haman, an advisor to Xerxes, the King of Persia. The day of the Jews' execution, a date determined randomly by the drawing of lots (*purim* in Hebrew), became instead a day of the destruction of their enemies. The written decree establishing the celebration of this holiday, recounted in chapter nine, upholds the recurring Old Testament theme of God's intervention to reverse the fortunes of the godly and the ungodly alike.

Clay Figure Playing a Pipe[8]
Figure 4.2 from the Ruins of Susa, capital of Persia under Xerxes

5

Instruments of Praise

Only when the ram's horn sounds a long blast may they go up to the mountain.
—Exodus 19:13 (NIV)

TO STUDY THE MUSICAL INSTRUMENTS of a different time and place in history is to study the very fabric of life, labor, ritual, and lament. The study of instruments of antiquity is as vast an endeavor as any other area of biblical exegesis, and scriptural evidence tells us much more about the instruments themselves and the occasions for their use than any evidence regarding vocal music. Predating the earliest *song* for which we have any actual evidence, the Hurrian cultic hymn to the goddess Nikal we noted in Chapter 1, are pictographic signs for a boat-shaped harp found on a Sumerian clay tablet from Uruk dating back to 3000 B.C., and an earlier depiction of this harp was found in modern southwest Iran dating ca. 3200 B.C.

The inspired word of God leaves us in no doubt as to the biblical father of musical instruments. According to the Scriptures, Jubal, son of Lamech of the line of Cain, was the father of harpists and organists. He was a brother of Jabal, a herdsman, and it was in the leisure of this nomadic occupation that music was first exercised and appreciated (Gen. 4:20–21). Soon thereafter Laban (the Syrian) mentions "songs, . . . tabret, and . . . harp" (Gen. 31:27 KJV).

The musical instruments referred to in the Bible fall into three groups—string, wind, and percussion. Unless otherwise noted, we will refer to the instruments with the names that the King James Version of the Bible uses and describe them in alphabetical order. (For a list of references to instruments in the Bible, see Appendix D.)

Stringed Instruments

We will sing my songs with stringed instruments all the days of our life.
—Isaiah 38:20 NKJV

Harp

Gen. 4:21; 1 Kgs. 10:12; Ps. 43:4; Rev. 5:8

Chief among the instruments, and the favorite of David, was the harp. Found more than fifty times in the Bible, it was used at both joyful and mournful ceremonies. When captives in Babylon, the Jews hung their harps on the willows in their dejection (Ps. 137:2). The prophets threatened that as a punishment for sin, the sound of the harp would cease (Isa. 24:8; Ezek. 26:13). The harp formed part of the instrumental music in the temple (1 Kgs. 10:12).

Kinnor, the Hebrew word for harp, is associated with the sound of the strings. Josephus distinguishes it as a ten-stringed instrument struck by a plectrum or played by the fingers. Original harps were light and could be played in processions or while dancing. Others were triangular in shape and held upright between the legs of a seated person. They consisted of a sound box at the base, two wooden side arms and a crossbar connected by the string to the box below. At first the strings were made of twisted grass or fibers of plants. Later they were formed of gut, and subsequently of silk and metal. In Solomon's time they were made from the algum tree, which is sometimes identified with sandalwood. Our beautiful modern harps with their resonant bodies are an evolution of elegant Egyptian harps, a favorite instrument of the cultured classes in Israel. Reference is made to both the smaller hand-held harp as played by walking prophets (1 Sam. 10:5), and the larger, many-stringed harp, played with plectrum or striker.

The music of the harp, as of other instruments, was raised to its highest perfection under David, who greatly excelled in its performance as he played it by hand (1 Sam. 16:23). It was the sweet music of the harp that often dispossessed Saul of his melancholy. We read that in David's hand there was a harp, but in Saul's hand a javelin or spear (1 Sam. 16:14–23; 18:10–11). What a contrast between these two instruments! Were they not symbolic of the different characters of David and Saul? David's hand played the harp; his was a melodious nature. Saul's hand held the spear; his was a murderous nature. The harp soothed. The spear slew. When will the nations learn that it is far more beneficial to play the harp than to hurl spears (2 Kgs. 3:13–17)?

When Isaiah wrote, "My heart laments for Moab like a harp," (Isa. 16:11 NIV), he was not alluding to any mournful or sorrowful sound but to the strings vibrating when struck. The prophet further uses the harp illustratively when he describes the desolation of Tyre: "Take up a harp, walk through the city, O prostitute forgotten; play the harp well, sing many a song, so that you will be remembered" (Isa. 23:16 NIV).

Harps are mentioned three times in the book of Revelation, and in each case they are associated with song. In earth's millennial praise, various musical instruments are named (Ps. 150), but the choral praise of the heavenly hosts is accompanied by the harp only, with harp and song in unison. The frequent use of the harp, more than any other instrument in ancient times, for the direct praise and worship of Jehovah was due to its rare combination of solemn, grand notes with soft and tender strains. In visions, John sees the saints and "each one ha[s] a harp" (Rev. 5:8 NIV). He also hears a sound "like that of harpists playing their harps" (Rev. 14:2 NIV). The redeemed celebrate God's intervention by mighty saving grace with song and harp (Rev. 5:8–10). Further, the apostle refers to two heavenly companies as having "harps given them by God" (Rev. 15:2 NIV). The words "by God" signify that the instruments, the only kinds mentioned in the Apocalypse, are provided by God for His direct praise and worship. They are God's harps, instruments, and musicians. No discord mars the harmony of heaven.

Lyre

The lyre is a stringed instrument of the harp class, richly wrought, and used by the ancient Greeks, especially in accompanying song and recitation. The lute is another stringed instrument with a large pear-shaped body, a long neck with a fretted fingerboard, and head with screws for tuning. It is played by plucking the strings with the fingers and is a development of the biblical harp. Various forms of stringed instruments sprang from this first named instrument in Scripture. No instrument in the King James Version of the Bible is referred to by the word "lyre." Instead, "harp" and "sackbut" are used.

Greek Music-Master Teaching a Youth to Play the Lyre[1]
Figure 5.1

Psaltery

1 Chr. 16:5; Ps. 71:22; 144:9; Dan. 3:5, 7, 10, 15

Young's concordance gives the meaning of the English term "psaltery," referred to almost thirty times in Scripture, as a "stringed instrument," "lyre," or "harp." From the Hebrew *nebel*, which means literally, a leather bottle, similar in shape to the psaltery (Ps. 92:3; 144:9), this instrument is another stringed instrument played by the hand to accompany the voice. David wrote, "Sing unto him with the psaltery and an instrument of ten strings" (Ps. 33:2 KJV). Josephus, the Jewish historian, says that ordinarily it had twelve strings and was played with a quill, not with the hand. Evidently it was an instrument that could be played to octaves. One writer suggests that it was like the guitar, a flat instrument, of a triangular form, and strung from side to side with wire.

The difference in the number of strings need not concern us, seeing there were harps of lesser and greater compass. The mention of the number of strings in two or three instances does not necessarily imply different kinds of harps. The number of the strings on the Assyrian harp ranges from sixteen upward, but there may have been fewer in some cases. David may have used a psaltery, "an instrument of ten strings" (KJV), as mentioned in Pss. 33:2, 92:3, and 144:9.

Sackbut

Dan. 3:5, 7, 10, 15

The prophet Daniel is the only one who mentions this harp-like instrument. Both the Hebrew and Greek refer to some form of harp, or lyre, but with only four strings, and one authority considers this to have been a form of flute rather than of harp. Yet scholars affirm that the English "sackbut" is a mistranslation. The sackbut is actually a wind instrument with a moveable slide, like the trombone. The musical instrument Daniel wrote about was a triangle with four strings, shrill and high in key.

Viol

Isa. 5:12; 14:11; Amos 5:23, 6:5

The Revised English Bible gives us "lute" for "viol" in Isa. 5:12. The Hebrew word here is *nebel,* also the one signified by psaltery. Probably there were several varieties of the *nebel,* and the viol, a small portable harp played with both hands, was one of them.

From Amos we learn of the melodious tone of the instrument (Amos 5:23). Isaiah's complaint was that a backsliding people could make and rejoice in their harps and viols, but were unable to regard the work of the Lord or consider the work of His hands (Isa. 5:12). We must not lose sight of the fact that the Hebrews fashioned their stringed instruments, not for their own self-satisfaction or for secular use, but primarily to glorify God who had planted music in their hearts.

Strings and voices, hands and hearts,
In the concert bear your parts:
All that breathe, your God adore,
Praise him, praise him evermore.[2]

Wind Instruments

"And the seven angels who had the seven trumpets prepared themselves to sound them." —Revelation 8:6 NASB

Cornet

2 Sam. 6:5; 1 Chr. 15:28; 2 Chr. 15:14; Ps. 98:6; Hos. 5:8
With three different Hebrew terms used for this English word "cornet," it is not easy to determine the exact kind of instrument meant, but we must not confuse the biblical references to this instrument with our modern cornet and its remarkable range. We have *keren,* the Hebrew word Daniel used in 3:5–15, referring to the primitive curved horn of a cow or ram. *Shophar* is the word found in 1 Chr. 15:28, 2 Chr. 15:14, Ps. 98:6, and Hos. 5:8. This was the long, straight horn turned up at the end, forming the national trumpet for rallying the people (see below under Trumpet).

In the psalter of the Anglican Book of Common Prayer (1662), cornet is given as "shawm," which is a bass instrument like the clarinet from the German schalmeie, a reed pipe with the compass of an octave and the tone of a bassoon, but plaintive.

Dulcimer

Dan. 3:5, 10, 15
The exact nature of this instrument, which Daniel alone mentions, is also not easy to determine. We place it among wind instruments, noting that archaeological research has clarified that this instrument is more accurately translated "bagpipe." Such an instrument "at one time was exceedingly popular, even among highly civilized peoples. Nero is said to be desirous of renown as a piper."[3] Supposedly this instrument

was like the Greek *symphonia,* which consisted of two pipes thrust through a leather bag, emitting a plaintive sound. Scottish bagpipes would appear to be a development of this instrument; however, others think the dulcimer was a flute or reed or the germ of the modern piano.

In modern use a dulcimer is a hollow triangular box strung with tightly stretched strings or wires of varying lengths, fixed by pins and turning screws over the box, and played by hammers struck with the hand against the strings.

Flute

Dan. 3:5, 7, 10, 15
The flute of today is a highly developed wind instrument and, in the hands of a skillful player, is able to produce a delightful range of tones. What Daniel, the only writer who mentions the flute, had in mind was doubtless a simpler form of its modern style. A mere tube with holes, played by blowing into one end or into a hole in the side, it may have been the panpipe, a kind of organ with various pipes, or a flageolet with two pipes. Of this we are certain: flute-like instruments date from the earliest times. In *The International Standard Bible Encyclopaedia,* James Millar reminds us:

> The flutes of the East and West resembled each other. . . . The Greeks, as their myths show, regarded Asia Minor as the birthplace of the flute, and no doubt the Hebrews brought it with them from their Assyr [*sic*] home. . . . It is apparently furnished with a beaked mouthpiece, like that of the clarinet or flageolet. We cannot determine whether the Israelites used the flute with a mouthpiece, or one like the nay [Arab flute], and it is futile to guess. It is enough to say that they had opportunities of becoming acquainted with both kinds, and may have adopted both.[4]

Horn

Josh. 6:5; 1 Chr. 25:5; Luke 1:69
Animal horns are referred to in different ways in Scripture. Often they are used figuratively (1 Sam. 2:1; 2 Sam. 22:3; Ps. 75:4; Dan.

7:7–24). The only aspects that concern us in this section are the methods of fashioning them and their employ as instruments. Rams' horns were blown on solemn occasions, and their use gave rise to the term "Jubilee," for the fiftieth year, the year of release or "the year of the ram's [horn]." Ram's horns were used to summon the people to praise God. "Trumpets of rams' horns" is translated as "trumpets of the jubilee" in Josh. 6:4–5 YLT). Instead of "to lift up the horn," the Revised Standard Version has "to exalt him" (1 Chr. 25:5). Finally, the Horn of Salvation proclaimed glorious victory over the enemy of souls. At first trumpets were perhaps merely horns perforated at the tips and were used for summoning to war or for public proclamations (Judg. 3:27; 7:18) or to announce important events (1 Kgs. 1:34, 39).

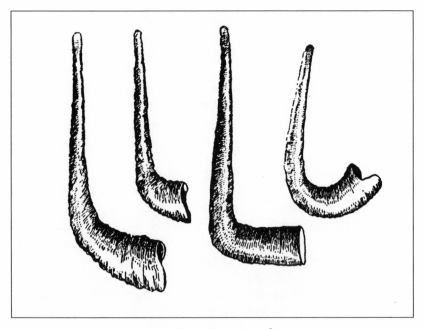

Samples of the *Shofar*[5]
Figure 5.2

The *shofar keren* was curved as an actual animal horn might be. These two Hebrew terms are used synonymously in Josh. 6:4–5, which can be translated "when the priests blow triumph on the horn." Doubtless much wind was required in blowing such a horn, and thus it did not produce attractive music. Nevertheless the people were certain as to its message when it was blown, especially when it heralded the approach of the ark or the ascension of a new king (2 Sam. 15:10). As horn is linked with trumpet, a fuller discussion will be found under Trumpet.

Organ

Gen. 4:21; Job 21:12; 30:31; Ps. 150:4

At the outset it must be made clear that the organ as we know it today, with its rich and varied music, was not known even in rudimentary form in Bible times. The Hebrew term *ugab,* meaning "to blow," rendered uniformly in the King James Version as "organ," became an obsolete word, as seen in the variety of renderings it has received. Jubal is the father of both the harp, a stringed instrument, and the organ, a wind instrument. Dr. Adam Clarke says it was probably the *syrinx,* "composed of several unequal pipes, close [*sic*] at the bottom, which when blown into at the top, gives a very shrill and lively sound."[6] The majority of scholars suggest that the organ was probably the bagpipe, an instrument of the highest antiquity and of very general use in the East. Young's concordance suggests it was a lute or flute.

Zondervan's Pictorial Bible Dictionary has a very interesting paragraph on the instrument in question:

> The organ *(megrepha)* was perhaps a primitive pneumatic [wind] organ and an advanced form of the ancient "ugab," mentioned in Gen. 4:21, which has for centuries been wrongly translated "organ." The organ was constructed of a skin-covered box with ten holes and each of them able to produce "ten kinds of songs," so that the whole organ was able to produce 100 "kinds of songs." It was used solely as a signal instrument to call the priests and the Levites to their duties. Its tone was very strong, the Mishna tells us, perhaps a little exaggerated; whenever the organ *(megrepha)* was played in the temple its sounds carried as far as Jericho.[7]

Whatever the nature of the instrument may have been, the people were exhorted to praise God with organs (Ps. 150:4), the main purpose of which was to magnify God as it was manipulated by wind and fingers to the limit of its capacity.

Poets have used the figure of the organ in most effective ways. John Milton (1608–1674), in his "Christ's Nativity," penned the stirring lines:

Ring out ye crystal spheres!
Once bless our human ears,
(If ye have power to touch our senses so)
And let your silver chime
Move in melodious time;
And let the bass of Heav'n's deep organ blow;
And with your ninefold harmony
Make up full consort to th'angelic symphony.
(8.125–132)

The word "organ" is from the Greek *organon*, meaning "an instrument," and having as a root *ergon*, meaning "work." It is from *ergon* that we have "energy," and from *organon*, "organism," or a group of organs dependent upon wind or air to function as a whole. The modern musical organ, when invented, worked with a bellows.

Pipe

1 Sam. 10:5; Jer. 48:36; Matt. 11:17; 1 Cor. 14:7

This English word "pipe" first referred to the piping sound and is most probably imitative of the flute in origin. The noun came to connote the shape of the musical instrument, just as the tube for smoking tobacco is called a pipe. Occurring some fifteen times in the Bible, "pipe" is used in a twofold way, namely, to describe a musical instrument such as a flute, and to refer to a utensil such as the two golden pipes of which Zechariah speaks (Zech. 4:12). Probably a shepherd's pipe or flute, this instrument is not found in the list associated with the temple. The Hebrew word for pipe is *ḥalil*, meaning "to bore," and the "shawm," of which the clarinet is an improvement, may derive from *ḥalil* through the French *chalumeau*. The pipe is the representative instrument of the wind instruments. It accompanied:

- Festivity (1 Kgs. 1:40; Isa. 5:12; Matt. 11:17; Luke 7:32)

- Religious services (1 Sam. 10:5)

- Processions (Isa. 30:29)

- Mourning (Jer. 48:36)

Israel and neighboring nations were familiar with reed pipes, as they were also with double flutes. However, the keyed flute was of later origin.

It is profitable to trace how the New Testament uses the pipe illustratively. Our Lord, in his condemnation of the Pharisees and lawyers, who rejected the counsel of God, asked the question, "Whereunto then shall I liken the men of this generation?" and went on to answer his own question: "They are like unto children sitting in the marketplace, and calling one to another, and saying, 'We have piped unto you, and ye have not danced; we have mourned to you, and ye have not wept.'" (Luke 7:31–32 KJV).

In his Nazareth home, Jesus had often watched the children playing at weddings and funerals, the village lads blowing long whistles. Here he makes full use of such an illustration. In Judea at weddings and feasts it was common to have lively music and dancing; at funerals, melancholy music and lamentations. Both feasts and funerals required a response, either by dancing or doleful notes, and if such was withheld, the complaint arose, "We have piped unto you, and ye have not danced," a complaint which became a proverb.

Interpreting the illustration in light of the context, the mourning airs in this proverb fitly represent the severity of John the Baptist's manners, as well as the disagreeableness of the doctrine of repentance that he preached. On the other hand, the more cheerful airs fittingly represent our Lord's sweet disposition: affable conversation and engaging method of giving instruction. Everything was tried that could possibly influence the Jews to repent and believe the gospel.

Paul likewise uses the illustration of the pipe with great effect:

Even things without life giving sound, whether pipe or harp, except they give a distinction in the sounds [tunes], how shall it be known what is piped or harped? For if the trumpet give an uncertain sound, who shall prepare himself to the battle? (1 Cor. 14:7–8 KJV)

As we have seen, the pipe and the harp were the best-known instruments among the Jews. Paul lays down the principle of the utter futility of sounds unless they are distinctive. The point of Paul's illustration is that each instrument has its own peculiar note or sound, and that each is known by the distinction of notes. If a trumpet does not clearly sound the advance when it is intended, or the retreat when it is meant, the trumpet is useless, the soldiers not knowing what to do. Paul then goes on to describe the varieties of human language produced by the tongue, the actual organ of speech. If in our presentation of the gospel, we do not use well-chosen words, how are those to whom we witness to understand? Such words pass as mere sounds into the air and are useless.

In his description of the irremediable destruction of Babylon, John writes that "the voice of harpers, and musicians, and of pipers, and trumpeters, shall be heard no more at all in thee" (Rev. 18:22). What utter desolation is poetically expressed by the apostle! Joyless, dark, and silent, Babylon stands out as a monument to the utmost vengeance of God. If the pipers are silent, heaven is not, for the call goes out:

> Rejoice over her, O heaven! Rejoice, saints and apostles and prophets! (Rev. 18:20 NIV)

Trumpet

Josh. 6:13, 16; Ps. 150:3; 1 Cor. 15:52; Rev. 8:2

The importance of the trumpet in Bible times is evidenced by the fact that "trumpet" and "trump," the abbreviation for trumpet, occur more than a hundred times, being used both literally and figuratively. Designed to produce loud sounds, the instrument in question was originally made of the long horn of a ram or ox and later of metal. The bugle, with which we are familiar, is a modern improvement of the Bible trumpet, which was used for rallying the people and rousing political or religious enthusiasm. In some verses it is rendered cornet (see Horn). The *shofar*, an ordinary small trumpet fashioned out of ram's horn, was curved and blown for a number of reasons.

Silver Trumpets

Num. 10:1–10

In this interesting passage, Moses is commanded to make two silver trumpets to be used for summoning the congregation and to be blown only by the priests. According to Josephus, these "silver" or metal trumpets were fashioned long, straight, and slender with a wide mouth and about one foot long. Quite distinctive from the "trumpet" or *shofar* made from animal horns, these silver instruments could not be handled by just anybody or by those of inferior rank.

The explicit command was: "The sons of Aaron, the priests, shall blow with the trumpets." When trumpets were blown in the appointed way, Israel was assured that she would be remembered before the Lord. Only the exalted sons of Aaron were privileged to blow the trumpets, and they did not deem such a task beneath their priestly function. Blowing trumpets may not seem a dignified office, but those trumpeters knew that the meanest office in the service of God is honorable and sacred. If they gave uncertain sounds, the people would be confused, so it was necessary for those priests to blow aright, or to reveal, by the tones of the instruments, the mind and purpose of God. The spiritual truth behind this particular priestly service was that the mind of God may be known and communicated only by those in priestly communion. Only such can know the correct note to strike, so that every member of the Lord's host can yield immediate, implicit obedience.

With the spiritual significance of the silver trumpets in Num. 10:1–10, it may be profitable to examine what Scripture says in this passage. Note that this portion follows instruction regarding the movement of the cloud (9:15–23). Both passages bear a striking likeness, which is as it should be because the guidance of the cloud and the sound of the trumpets illustrate that presence and proclamation go together. The notes of the silver trumpets were familiar to every Israelite ear; the Israelites depended upon the movement of the cloud and the music of the trumpet. Such formed the communication of God's mind in a simple way and were as easily understandable as a soldier listening for different bugle notes. As the trumpets were the voice of God to the whole of Israel, the priests took care that the vast assembly heard the notes.

Although these instruments were bound up in a marked way with the entire history of Israel, past and future, there are a few facts about the trumpets illustrative of the gospel we preach. The eye of faith can see several important truths in connection with the voice of God to our own age.

Number

"Make thee two trumpets of silver." Why were there only two trumpets fashioned by Moses? The simple answer is that only two priests were alive at that time. Nadab and Abiha had died before the Lord (Num. 3:1–4). In Solomon's time there were 120 priests set aside for the task of blowing the silver trumpets (2 Chr. 5:12). The two, then, can typify unity of testimony and harmony in witness. "How can two walk together, except they be agreed?" "If two of you shall agree." The Lord Jesus combined most perfectly two natures in one person.

Unity

"Of a whole piece shalt thou make them." As we have indicated, each of these trumpets was a long straight tube of silver with a bell-shaped mouth. They were not cast in a mold, but made of beaten work and had no joints or additions. Being of one piece, they spoke of unity. Is this not so with Scripture? While its theme may vary, its source of testimony is one. How assuring is this characteristic feature of harmony!

Then, can we not apply the phrase, "whole piece" to Him who is the living word? He was not cast in any set mold, but was beaten work. Upon the anvil of temptation, sorrow and death, He was fashioned into our silver trumpet.

Nature

"Two silver trumpets." The Jewish historian, Josephus, says, of the silver trumpets:

> In length it was little less than a cubit. It was composed of a narrow tube, somewhat thicker than a flute, but with so much breadth . . . for admission of the breath . . . it ended in the form of a bell like the common trumpets. (*Antiquities* 3.12.6)

Moses fashioned them according to the pattern of the mount. It is a known fact that silver instruments give the sweetest music, therefore being made of silver not only made them precious but imparted sweetness of tone. The Bible, God's silver trumpet, revolves around the cross of Christ. All types, symbols, and prophecies focus upon the great central truth of the atoning work of Calvary, a work both precious and sweet of tone.

Purpose

"For the calling of the assembly, and for the journeying of the camps." Every movement of the host was governed by the sound of the silver trumpets. Not a step was taken until the silvery sound of the instrument was heard. The fact that priests alone handled them indicates that their use was sacred rather than martial. Every forward march was governed by the blowing of the trumpets. The first blast by the priest actually meant, "Come," and the second blast said, "Go!" God said to Noah, "Come into the ark," and after the flood the command was, "Go forth and replenish." Jesus said, "Come unto me and rest," and then, "Go you into all the world." As the redeemed of the Lord we dare not move apart from divine direction. Indeed, our every step must be ordered by Him. As the trumpets ordered every action of Israel, so the word of God should order or settle everything for the child of God.

Percussion Instruments

The sound of the bells will be heard when he enters the Holy Place.
—Exodus 28:35 (NIV)

Percussion instruments are those producing tones by being struck in various ways. Percussion comes from a root that means "to shake," an action necessary if a tambourine is to function. An impressive feature of the musical instruments of the Bible, whether string, wind, or percussion, is that they were the foundation of the more intricate and highly varied tonal instruments used by bands and orchestras today.

The evolution of musical instruments is an absorbing study in itself, and much scholarly, exegetical, and archaeological work has been done in this area. In this section, we are but skimming the surface of a broad and thorough endeavor. The music produced by ancient instruments was of a monotonous nature, and by no means as melodious as that to which we are accustomed. However, we do know that the general nature of ancient Hebrew music was quite likely diatonic (any musical scale consisting of five tones and two semitones such as a major or minor scale with no sharps or flats) and tetrachordal (a group of four notes, the first and last of which form a perfect fourth). In Bible days, percussion instruments were elemental in nature and of limited variety.

Bells

Exod. 28:33–34; 39:25–26; Zech. 14:20
Music is obtained from bells by striking them, and such a percussion instrument can be considered one of humankind's first musical instruments. Over four thousand years ago the Chinese had an instrument consisting of sixteen flat stones suspended in a frame, which gave forth a scale of exotic notes when struck by a wooden mallet.

Legend has it that King Solomon had large gold bells on the roof of the temple he built to keep the birds away. Doubtless in Bible times small bells were fastened to the necks of goats and sheep, thereby facilitating the shepherd's task of judging their whereabouts. Zechariah mentions bells around the necks of horses (Zech. 14:20). A number of small bronze bells, both of the ordinary shape with clapper and of the "ball and slit" form, were unearthed several years ago at Gezer.

Small bells for tinkling purposes were attached to the hem of the priestly robes worn by Aaron and his sons as they performed their priestly service in the tabernacle. Hearing the little bells assured the worshipers that the high priest had not incurred divine retribution but remained alive as their intercessor.

The custom of using large bells to summon worshipers to church is a Christian practice Bishop Paulinus is supposed to have introduced in the fourth century A.D. The Hebrew word for "bell" means "to strike." The tinkling ornaments women wore about their feet were likely tiny bells designed to attract attention (Isa. 3:16, 18, 20). A different Hebrew term is used for the bells on the horses (Zech. 14:20). Here, small shells of brass, like castanets, were fastened to the horses' harnesses. Their jingling enlivened the animals and kept them aware of one another.

Cymbals

2 Sam. 6:5; 1 Chr. 16:5, 42; Ps. 150:5; 1 Cor. 13:1

The word "cymbal" is from a root meaning "to tingle" or "tinkle." Evidently there were two kinds. The first were loud cymbals or castanets made up of four small plates of brass. Two plates were attached to each hand and smitten together, marking for the choir their time for joining in the sacred song (1 Chr. 13:8). The second were high-sounding cymbals. These consisted of two larger plates, one held in each hand, and struck together as an accompaniment to other music, like the Italian *piatti,* marking the rhythm. Present day cymbals are manipulated in this way. God was to be praised with both forms (Ps. 150:5). In the Hebrew, the name cymbal generally occurs in the dual number, showing that a pair of them was used.

In Bible days, cymbals, the only permanent percussion instrument used in the temple orchestra, were solely confined to religious ceremonies, as can be seen from the following occasions:

- The return of the ark (1 Chr. 15:16, 19, 28)

- The dedication of Solomon's temple (2 Chr. 5:12–13)

- The restoration of divine worship by Hezekiah (2 Chr. 29:25)

- The laying of the foundation of the second temple (Ezra 3:10)

- The dedication of the wall of Jerusalem (Neh. 12:27)

During the reigns of David and Solomon much stress was laid upon the playing of the cymbals and percussion instruments in assemblies and processions. Asaph, David's chief singer, was a cymbal-player (1 Chr. 16:5). Also popular in Egypt, a pair of cymbals made of copper and silver were found in a grave at Thebes. They were about five inches in diameter, having handles fixed in the center.

Paul used the figure of the cymbal in a most effective way: "If I speak in the tongues of men and of angels, but have not love, I am only a resounding gong or a clanging cymbal" (1 Cor. 13:1 NIV). Francis Bacon, in his essay "Of Friendship," uses the same figure of speech: "A crowd is not company; and faces are but a gallery of pictures; and talk but a tinkling cymbal, where there is no love." In his hymn honoring true love, love to God and man, Paul shows that the most glorious gifts are nothing without the more excellent way of love. The gifts may be exercised, but there will be only sound without soul or feeling.

Sistrum

2 Sam. 6:5 NIV

This noise-making instrument, similar in shape to an old-fashioned sling-shot, was made with a bent rod of iron in a horseshoe shape with cross bars on which rings were placed, so that it rattled when shaken. The term *menanaim* appears only once (2 Sam. 6:5). In translation, the RSV and NRSV give us "castanets," and the margin suggests *sistra,* or the *sistrum,* a kind of rattle that was very common in the East. The ancient Egyptians jingled this metallic instrument, with its light frame and transverse metal rods, in their ceremonies associated with the worship of Isis. The word *sistra* means "to shake." The loose rings, threaded on the crossbars of metal rods, jingled when shaken, like the plates of a timbrel. Thus, the instrument mentioned only in this passage of Samuel and translated in the KJV as "cornets" was actually not a stringed instrument as the psaltery and the harp. The cornet of David that made "a joyful noise before the LORD" (Ps. 98:6) was a hand-shaken rattle.

Tabret

Judg. 11:34; Pss. 68:25; 150:4

The Hebrew *toph* is used for the tabret and also the timbrels (Gen. 31:27; Job 21:12). This instrument resembled the modern tambourine and was used with cymbals as an accompaniment to dancing and singing. It was formed of a circular frame of wood about ten inches in diameter, covered with a piece of skin tightly drawn over it, sometimes surrounded with small bells and struck with the hand. Hence, there arose the expression, "tabering upon their breasts," that is, women beating their breasts in sorrow as they would beat a tabret or tambourine as an expression of lament (Nah. 2:7). An accompaniment to the pipe, this drum-like instrument was the forerunner of the large and small drums now used in bands.

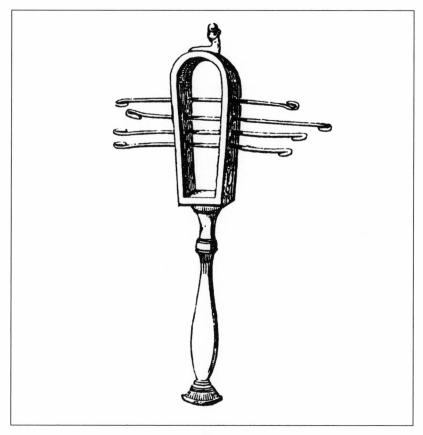

Sistrum[8]
Figure 5.3 from the Berlin Museum

While both "tabret" and "timbrel" are representatives of the Hebrew *toph*, they are yet of different origin in English. "Tabret" is derived
from the Arabic *tanbur*, a sort of mandolin, while "timbrel" comes
from the Latin/Greek *tympanium*, through the French *timbre*, meaning
"a small tambourine" or hand drum. The Old English *tabor* signifies a
drum.

PART 2

■　　■　　■

Hymns, Psalms, and Spiritual Songs

6

The Significance of Hebrew Poetry

He restores my soul. —Psalm 23:3 (NIV)

WE HAVE TRAVERSED the history of ancient music through the rich stories of Abraham who set out on a journey of faith; Miriam who trusted that God would provide; Moses who led the wandering tribes; Deborah and Barak who provided spiritual leadership in a war-faring land; and Hannah, whose life of fervent prayer brought forth a son named Samuel, a prophet and judge whose spiritual leadership prepared the way for rag-tag tribes to become a united kingdom. From the Hebrews' dramatic escape out of Egypt to the walls of Jericho falling to the sounds of priests' *shofars* and drums, music in the Bible is woven through the history of ancient Israel as indelibly as the notes and staffs in a musical masterpiece.

Approaching the subject before us, sublime and sacred as it is, we have to confess that no saint can fully explain the intrinsic role of music in the history of the people of God, though many have tried. Vast amounts of scholarship, study, exposition, and analysis have contributed to our understanding of music in ancient Israel and its frequent mention in Scripture. Indeed, one Jewish historian has noted, "Throughout the ancient history of the Jewish people . . . we find music mentioned with a frequency that perhaps exceeds that of its mention in the history of any other people."[1] Such literature is most extensive; we must, therefore, acknowledge the brevity of a study of this nature in contrast to the riches of the resources available to those endeavoring to study the far-reaching ramifications of music in the Bible.

Nonetheless, this study you hold before you constitutes a personal endeavor to express in simple terms for believers the manifold mysteries of God through music, poetry, and song. Yet one must keep in mind that though we can personally experience the power of music, a true understanding of its mystery may well exceed our grasp. I am, therefore, compelled to say that any exposition of the qualities and characteristics of music in the Bible is more or less imperfect because of our inability to fully describe the divine role in salvation history that music has played. (For a list of well-known songs in the Bible, see Appendix B; for songs in the Bible that are mentioned only by name, see Appendix C.)

With these limitations acknowledged, we now turn our attention to songs from books of the Bible that are largely poetic in form, a significant transition for one very simple reason: Of the thirty-nine books of the Old Testament, works of "expansive narratives and short stories, legal codes [and] historical reports, hymns and prayers . . . proverbs, maxims . . . riddles . . . [and] mysterious revelations,"[2] *fully one third* of this diverse Holy Book is poetry. Think of the significance of this fact! From the Torah or Law given to the emerging nation of Israel, to the books known as the Writings, the recorded history of the people of God, to the Prophets (the last seventeen books of the Old Testament), *fully one third of this comes to us in poetic form.* Obviously, herein lies a treasure trove of biblical significance! Only seven Old Testament books contain no poetic lines: Leviticus, Ruth, Ezra, Nehemiah, Esther, Haggai, and Malachi. Much of Jesus' teaching was expressed by quoting Old Testament poetry. To approach the songs of David, or delve into the riches of the Psalms or the compelling words of Isaiah without a few comments on the nature of Hebrew poetry itself would be a regrettable omission.

The form of Hebrew poetry, a fascinating and expansive study itself, is quite distinctive from the nursery-rhyme balance of sound and rhythm with which we find ourselves most familiar. Poetry of the ancient Hebrews was not written with rhyme and rhythm being primary factors. In fact, rhyme and rhythm are virtually non-existent, appearing only occasionally (Isa. 41:11–13 being one example). No, the distinguishing, fundamental feature of the poetry in the Old Testament is that of parallelism, a balance of thought rather than sound. The poet writes one line of thought, followed by another line of thought parallel to the first, a poetic form progressing through successive half-lines.

The thought may be repeated, contrasted, or advanced. A biblical scholar credited with first advancing the study of this feature of Hebrew poetry documented at least seven different types of parallelism.

The lack of rhythm and rhyme in the words of the psalmists and prophets is not experienced as a loss of lyrical quality in the Hebrew language. As the words were originally rendered in Hebrew, the effect was one of explosive, staccato, sounds and powerful, memorable repetitions. The Word of God as it was given, the miracle of salvation history as it was told, came in a language and form that carried forcefulness, impact, and urgency. If we are tempted to think that the poetic form of Old Testament Scriptures is less than compelling, we must think again. The line between poet and prophet, lyricist and historian, divine revelation and moving melody, is a thin line indeed, as is the line between poem and song, hymn and psalm. Because the line between what was originally musical and that which was poetic is difficult for us to know with certainty, we will severely restrict our study of the songs of Kings and Prophets to several specific texts, recognizing nonetheless that a study of song and poem in the Old Testament could easily become a life-long endeavor.

7

Songs of King David

Next to theology, I give music the highest place and honor. And we see how David and all the saints have wrought their godly thoughts into verse, rhyme and song. —Martin Luther

King David

PERHAPS NO OTHER MAN in the Old Testament so captures our imaginations as David, the mighty ruler, the anointed one, the second and unarguably the most powerful king of ancient Israel. Yet this servant of God began his life as a shepherd boy, a simple and lowly station in life. As sheep quietly grazed on the countryside tended by an unassuming young Hebrew from the tribe of Judah, a talented young musician emerged from this solitary life. David's early life was inseparable from the sounds of nature, the music of harp and lyre, the serenades that no doubt became the basis for songs David composed later in his life. Many of the Psalms are David's enduring legacy. Yet more than a talented musician emerged from those humble beginnings. David learned the ways of the desert, the rhythms of sun and seasons, the ebb and flow of rushing *wadis*,[1] the harsh realities of a rugged land. David came to know the land of ancient Israel in the same way we memorize the details of a loved one's face. His early life in the hills surrounding Bethlehem prepared him for a time when he would be called upon to serve as a leader, a military strategist, and a courageous man of prayer and war.

The youngest of the eight sons of Jesse, David was born in Bethlehem and began his reign as king when he was only thirty years old. His life spanned the simplicity of a shepherd's hillside to the opulence of a palace. From humble beginnings of lowly rank in the little town of Bethlehem to the greatest king of Israel, it pleased God to raise him from a low estate and set him on the throne. Initially overlooked by his father, Jesse, he was nonetheless chosen to be king when God said to the prophet Samuel, "Arise, anoint him: for this is he" (1 Sam. 16:12 KJV). Volumes have been written about the trials and triumphs of David, a man freely chosen "after [God's] own heart" (1 Sam. 13:14 NIV), but here we offer a brief sketch of David's eventful life, and in so doing, we will see how consistently music, song, and lyric were woven like golden threads through his life.

Warrior

From the days of his youth, David was courageous. When the Israelites were frozen with fear by the intimidation and threats of Goliath, David asked the question, "For who is this uncircumcised Philistine that he should defy the armies of the living God?" (1 Sam. 17:26 NRSV). Cautioned by Saul, "You are not able to go against this Philistine . . . for you are just a boy" (1 Sam. 17:33 NRSV), David confidently asserted that since he could kill lions and bears that threatened his sheep, how much more confidently he could overpower this warrior who defied the Lord of hosts. Not yet a man and lacking any training as a soldier, David had faith in the "name of the LORD" (1 Sam. 17:45 NRSV). Never were two opponents more unequally matched. Carrying only his staff, his sling, and five smooth stones in his shepherd's pouch, David claimed victory over the giant. There was no empty boasting, no reliance on his own power and might. David's confidence was in the Lord, and the battle between the young David and the mighty Goliath established David as one on whom God's favor shone.

Prophet

David possessed a prophetic gift given to only a few. With the inspiration of the Holy Spirit, this holy man revealed glorious truths related to Christ as Savior and Messiah. The New Testament quotes the psalms of David more frequently than it does any other part of the Old Testament.

Saint

David was dedicated and brought to a place of prominence as a man of God. From Samuel's declaring David "a man after [God's] own heart" (1 Sam. 13:14 NIV), to Saul's declaring to David, "You are more righteous than I" (1 Sam. 24:17 NIV), we are told repeatedly in 1 and 2 Samuel, "The LORD is with him." Unlike Saul, who became king because the Israelites insisted on having a king, David was God's own choice to rule over His people. David's psalms of praise, worship and meditation clearly indicate he possessed the qualities of a saint, made all the more poignant and relevant for today's Christian by his moral failings, jealousy, and greed as well. The story of David is the story of God at work in our lives and what can happen when we surrender our wills and lives to God's righteousness.

Musician

Before David became king, he often found himself in the presence of King Saul due to his skills as harpist and lyricist. Only the calming melodies of David's harp could subdue Saul's torment and rage. Blessed with poetic genius, David's majestic psalms of praise and movingly poignant laments are masterpieces in spiritual literature. Written most often for specific life situations or crises, these psalms were composed lyrically, vividly, and honestly, capturing David's own feelings as well as timeless emotions and eternal truths that resonate with us still today.

As a musician, David stands apart for another historical accomplishment credited to his leadership. Before the time of David, music was not organized for the purposes of corporate worship and praise. Prior to David's rule, music was a spontaneous response, often led by women as they sang, danced and performed. David, visionary that he was, saw the value of organizing professional musicians.

The importance of a large class of professional musicians in any nation is evident: fixed scales, tunes, rhythms, and common practices tend to be developed and codified. Under King David, out of 38,000 Levites, 4,000 were appointed as musicians (1 Chr. 23:5).

First Chronicles also records that, "David . . . set apart some of the sons of Asaph, Heman and Jeduthun for the ministry of prophesying, accompanied by harps, lyres and cymbals . . . along with their relatives—all of them trained and skilled in music for the LORD—they numbered 288" (1 Chr. 25:1, 7 NIV).

Asaph was one of four chief musicians during David's reign and most likely the author of Pss. 50 and 73–83. Heman, another chief musician, was the grandson of Samuel and authored Ps. 88, often called the "darkest psalm in the psalter" because of its despairing lament. Jeduthun and Ethan round out this quartet. Ethan wrote Ps. 89. Other musicians included Benaiah and Jahaziel, who were daily trumpeters and performed before the Ark of the Covenant in the tabernacle (1 Chr. 16:6). Still others conducted grand musical services when the Ark was moved from the house of Obed-Edom to Jerusalem (1 Chr. 15:22).

The Songs of David

Though David's legacy is often thought to be the Psalms, several of his songs appear much earlier in the Old Testament. It is to these we turn first.

Lament over Saul and Jonathan

Also remembered as "The Song of the Bow," this intensely personal song is one of the Bible's earliest poems. Following the deaths of Saul and Jonathan, David sang this song of lament out of deep sorrow and grief which is evident in the emotion of his words. We are told, "David took hold of his clothes and tore them; and all the men who were with him did the same. They mourned and wept, and fasted until evening for Saul and for his son Jonathan" (2 Sam. 1:11–12 NRSV). In verse 18, David ordered that "The Song of the Bow" be taught to the people of

Judah. "How the mighty have fallen" in verses 19, 25, and 27 sets the theme for this lament and becomes the refrain for this song.

Your glory, O Israel, lies slain upon your high places!
How the mighty have fallen!

Tell it not in Gath, proclaim it not in the streets of Ashkelon;
or the daughters of the Philistines will rejoice,
the daughters of the uncircumcised will exult.

You mountains of Gilboa, let there be no dew or rain upon you,
nor bounteous fields! For there the shield of the mighty was
defiled, the shield of Saul, anointed with oil no more.

From the blood of the slain, from the fat of the mighty, the bow
of Jonathan did not turn back, nor the sword of Saul return
empty.

Saul and Jonathan, beloved and lovely! In life and in death they
were not divided; they were swifter than eagles, they were
stronger than lions.

O daughters of Israel, weep over Saul, who clothed you with
crimson, in luxury, who put ornaments of gold on your
apparel.

How the mighty have fallen in the midst of the battle!

Jonathan lies slain upon your high places. I am distressed for
you, my brother Jonathan; greatly beloved were you to me;
your love to me was wonderful, passing the love of women.

How the mighty have fallen, and the weapons of war perished!
(2 Sam. 1:19–27 NRSV)

Song of Victory

From his shepherding days until his death, David had the heart and soul of a warrior, a heart of courage and compassion and a mind both bold and shrewd. Under David's leadership, strategic military battles were won, warring tribes brought to peace, and political disputes resolved. David's encounter with Goliath was only the beginning of facing foes and gaining victory. In all things, David bowed before God and eagerly praised Him for many victories.

David's song of victory in 2 Sam. 22:2–51 (preserved in a very similar version in Ps. 18) is an excellent example of parallelism and repetition. In the first two verses of this lengthy song, powerful words conjuring images of God's strength and saving power are used eleven times: rock, fortress, deliverer, refuge, shield, salvation, stronghold, savior, not including the verb form of "saved."

Is it not safe to say that the repetition of these strong, vivid words foreshadow the very characteristics of our Lord and Savior Jesus Christ? And is it any wonder that Jesus himself used the word "rock" (Greek, *petros*) when saying to Peter, "and on this rock I will build my church" (Matthew 16:18 NRSV)? It is worthy of note that Jesus' words to Peter are one of only two times the word "church" is found in the Gospels; the second is Matt. 18:17. If it be true that the Bible is the Living Word of God and the Word of the Lord is meant to be heard, then read these few lines out loud for the edification of your spirit. For after all, poetry, like good sermons, is made in the hearing.

The LORD is my rock, my fortress, and my deliverer,

my God, my rock, in whom I take refuge,
my shield and the horn of my salvation,
my stronghold and my refuge,
my savior; you save me from violence.

I call upon the LORD, who is worthy to be praised,
and I am saved from my enemies.
(2 Sam. 22:2–4 NRSV)

What follows these opening lines are 49 verses of magnificent praise for God's deliverance. The song is written in two distinct sections. Verses 2–20 are David's praise for deliverance; verses 30–43 describe what a God can do with a willing and righteous man; verses 21–29 connect the two. The song comes to its conclusion in verses 44–51, extolling the God of deliverance while proclaiming David the "anointed" one.

The LORD lives! Blessed be my rock, and exalted be my God, the rock of my salvation, the God who gave me vengeance and brought down peoples under me,

who brought me out from my enemies; you exalted me above my adversaries, you delivered me from the violent.

For this I will extol you, O LORD, among the nations, and sing praises to your name.

He is a tower of salvation for his king, and shows steadfast love to his anointed, to David and his descendants forever.
(2 Sam. 22:47–51 NRSV)

The Dancing of David

One of the greatest moments of David's life occurred when he transported the Ark of the Covenant to its permanent place in a tabernacle near his palace (2 Sam. 6; 1 Chr. 15:1). The Ark contained tablets of the Ten Commandments, Aaron's rod, and a pot of manna and was the most sacred object in ancient worship, a symbol marking the presence of the Lord in much the same way as the Bible on the altar of most churches signifies the presence of the Living Word in worship today.

As the Levites conveyed the Ark to its new house, the Israelites processed in celebration. David led the celebration amid wild dancing and celebratory music:

David and all the house of Israel were dancing before the LORD with all their might, with songs and lyres and harps and tambourines and castanets and cymbals. (2 Sam. 6:5 NRSV)

Again, verses 14 and 16 in 2 Sam. 6 describe David "leaping and dancing" before the Lord. When Saul's daughter Michal attempted to shame and ridicule David for such an excessive display, David defended his actions by saying, "It was before the LORD, who chose me in place of your father . . . that I have danced before the LORD." David's understanding of the power of music, song, and unrestrained praise would not be tempered!

Men Dancing to a Rhythmic Instrument as a Woman Looks On[2]
Figure 7.1 from an Egyptian engraving

Song of Thanksgiving

As soon as the celebration had come to an end and the Ark had reached its resting place, David offered sacrifices to the Lord. He then instructed the Levites to summon the people of Israel and teach them this psalm of thanksgiving.

One need not be a student of great literature or a renowned Biblical scholar to observe that several themes run through the Bible like rivers running through the desert. These major themes can be divided into two categories. The first are themes revealing how the Almighty God of history acts in the story of His people: covenant, salvation, deliverance, leadership, wisdom, and hope. The second are themes telling us who God is, yesterday, today, and forever: God's faithfulness, sovereignty, and righteousness.

David's song of thanksgiving as recorded in 1 Chronicles draws from three different psalms (105:1–15; 96; 106:1, 47–48) and in 26 strongly worded verses, David's poetic genius captures all of these major themes. I consider it well advised to pause, open your Bible and read this moving song of praise aloud. Only in so doing can one come to hear the bass tones of active verbs pulsing through the praise. In these 26 verses, at least 46 active verbs appear, depending on which translation is before you. Sing, tell, declare, remember, seek, rejoice, come, give, gather—these are but a few of the verbs that leap off the page. Can we not hear the power of this song of praise in a few of the opening and closing lines?

> O give thanks to the LORD, call on his name, make known his deeds among the peoples.
>
> Sing to him, sing praises to him, tell of all his wonderful works.
>
> Glory in his holy name; let the hearts of those who seek the LORD rejoice.
>
> Seek the LORD and his strength, seek his presence continually.
>
> Remember the wonderful works he has done, his miracles, and the judgments he uttered,
>
> O offspring of his servant Israel, children of Jacob, his chosen ones.
>
> Ascribe to the LORD, O families of the peoples, ascribe to the LORD glory and strength.
>
> Ascribe to the LORD the glory due his name; bring an offering, and come before him. Worship the LORD in holy splendor;
>
> tremble before him, all the earth. The world is firmly established; it shall never be moved.
>
> Let the heavens be glad, and let the earth rejoice, and let them say among the nations, "The LORD is king!"
>
> Let the sea roar, and all that fills it; let the field exult, and everything in it.
>
> Then shall the trees of the forest sing for joy before the LORD, for he comes to judge the earth.

O give thanks to the LORD, for he is good; for his steadfast love endures forever.

Say also: "Save us, O God of our salvation, and gather and rescue us from among the nations, that we may give thanks to your holy name, and glory in your praise.

Blessed be the LORD, the God of Israel, from everlasting to everlasting." Then all the people said "Amen!" and praised the LORD.
(1 Chr. 16:8–13, 28–36 NRSV)

It is a worthwhile exercise, indeed, to take this song, verse by verse, and list the verbs from each. After such a study, one can easily see why it is no wonder that David danced without restraint!

8

The Psalter
Hymnbook of the Hebrews

*[The Psalter serves] to teach us the true method of praying aright . . . there is no
other book in which we are more perfectly taught in the right manner of praising God. . . . [the psalms] teach and train us to bear the cross.*[1]
—John Calvin

TO OPEN THE BIBLE to the book of Psalms is to see vivid metaphors and
picturesque images leaping off of its pages. The "varied and resplen-
dent riches"[2] of the psalms carry readers and listeners to spiritual
heights with rich word pictures, such as those comparing the godly
person to "a tree planted by streams of water, which yields its fruit in
season and whose leaf does not wither" (Ps. 1:3 NIV). Petition, praise,
worship, repentance, and thankfulness stream forth from the psalms,
revealing a private and communal piety expressed from deep within
the human heart. No wonder the Hebrew name for the book of Psalms,
sefer tehillim, means "the book of praises." The hope expressed therein
has sustained the spirits of the people of God throughout the ages during times of crisis and suffering.

Indeed, as John Calvin so aptly writes in the Preface to his
commentary:

[The Psalms are] an anatomy of all parts of the soul, for there is
not an emotion of which any one can be conscious that is not here
represented as in a mirror. Or rather, the Holy Spirit has here
drawn to the life all the griefs, sorrows, fears, doubts, hopes, cares,

perplexities, in short, all the distracting emotions with which the minds of men are wont to be agitated.[3]

This diverse collection of ancient Hebrew poetry comprises the longest book of the Bible and contains some of the best-known, most well loved pages in all of Scripture. Also called the "worship book of Israel," the psalms are thought to be "a microcosm of the Bible as a whole" which "mirrors the broad spectrum of human experience." One Bible teacher has said of the psalms that "few parts of the Bible have been taken more into the memory of mind and the literature of culture" than the psalms.[4]

The Hebrews sang and recited hymns to remind them that justice and righteousness are cornerstones of God's rule: that a moral law exists; God is faithful to His character; and God uses His sovereign control to unfold history. Nehemiah, a leader of the ancient Hebrews who returned to Jerusalem from Babylon to rebuild her walls, wrote:

> At the dedication of the wall of Jerusalem, the Levites were sought out from where they lived and were brought to Jerusalem to celebrate joyfully the dedication with songs of thanksgiving and with the music of cymbals, harps and lyres. . . . I had the leaders of Judah go up on top of the wall. I also assigned two large choirs to give thanks. (Neh. 12:27, 31 NIV)

The ancient Hebrews' hymns were eventually collected into what became the Psalter, known today as the book of Psalms. A collection of poems, songs, and prayers written over a period of time spanning centuries and compiled for both communal worship and personal piety, the psalms emphasize truths that remain relevant and penetrating, even today.

The Psalter provides encouragement, comfort, and peace. Its majestic poetry meets the needs of believers caught in life's difficult hours. Its words guide people, who face the future with fear, into the hope that only God can bring. As Martin Luther so movingly wrote:

> Where does one find finer words of joy than in the Psalms of praise and thanksgiving? There you look into the hearts of all saints . . . yes, as into heaven itself. . . . On the other hand, where do you find deeper, more sorrowful, more pitiful words of sadness than in the

Psalms of lamentation? There again you look into the hearts of all the saints, as into death, yes, as into hell itself. How gloomy and dark it is there. . . . And that they speak these words to God and with God, this, I repeat, is the best thing of all.[5]

Many of us only need to think of particular psalms, or portions of psalms, that have touched our lives today in order to imagine how greatly these hymns must have influenced the ancient Hebrews' lives. To recognize the Psalter's impact throughout the centuries would be to recall countless harvests reaped from its words.

It's no wonder! The Psalter reveals so much about the faith and history of Israel and helps readers form a biblical theology emphasizing God's covenantal relationship with His people. Clearly the book of Psalms comprises a vital portion of the Holy Scriptures. In fact, even during Jesus' day the apostles viewed the book of Psalms as prophetic and quoted from it extensively. Jesus reminded the apostles,

Everything must be fulfilled that is written about me in the Law of Moses, the Prophets and the Psalms. (Luke 24:44 NIV)

Since the founding of the Church, faithful Christians have chanted the Psalter in liturgy. Today's congregations still use responsive readings based on the psalms, and many of our most enduring hymns come directly from the psalms, such as "A Mighty Fortress Is Our God" (Ps. 46:1), "O God, Our Help in Ages Past" (Ps. 90:1), and "The King of Love My Shepherd Is" (Ps. 23).

In order to understand the music of the Bible, we must understand more about the Psalter, the hymnbook of the ancient Hebrews.

Writers of the Psalms

Many people typically associate the book of Psalms with David, *the* psalmist. Yet fewer than half (73) of the 150 psalms bear his name in their introductory notes. Asaph is credited with 12 psalms, the sons of Korah are associated with eleven; two bear Solomon's name; and Heman the Ezrahite, Ethan the Ezrahite, and Moses are credited with one each. The remaining authors are anonymous.

As stated, various psalms are credited to Asaph, a choirmaster who played cymbals before the ark of the Lord (1 Chr. 16:4–7; Pss. 50, 73–83). Scripture reveals that his descendants played a key role as singers (Ezra 2:41). Other psalms (42, 44–49, 84–85, 87–88) are associated with the sons of Korah, descendants of the Levite who rebelled during the wilderness wandering and was "swallowed up" by the earth (Num. 16:1–34; 26:10–11). According to 2 Chr. 20:19, "Some Levites from the Kohathites and Korahites stood up and praised the LORD, the God of Israel, with very loud voice" (NIV). Finally, as we have seen, the highest number of psalms bear the name of King David.

Did David write all of the 73 psalms attributed to him? We don't know, since we cannot pinpoint exactly when each psalm or collection of psalms was written and which author wrote them. However, the psalms often portray a worshiper who is struggling with powerful enemies, and David certainly experienced that type of conflict with King Saul and his troops. Also, the Davidic psalms contain a poetic quality that one might associate with a gifted person such as David who had deep spiritual faith and much creativity.

Five Books of the Psalter

Concerning God's revelation and his purposes, the entire book of Psalms is one unit. Yet, this book has been arranged into five distinct divisions, perhaps existing independently prior to the binding of the entire collection. Let's explore each hymnbook briefly.

Hymnbook One: Psalms 1–41

Known as the "David-Jehovah Psalms," these magnify God as Jehovah, the name by which God told Moses to call Him. (The word Jehovah is used 279 times; Elohim is used 45 times.) They are thought by many to have been authored by David. The doxology or closing praise to this collection is found in Ps. 41:13:

Praise be to the LORD, the God of Israel, from everlasting to everlasting. Amen and Amen. (NIV)

Hymnbook Two: Psalms 42–72

These 31 psalms are known as the "Elohim Psalms" because the divine name Elohim, which refers to God the wonder-worker, is used 262 times. Eighteen of the psalms are attributed to David, seven to the sons of Korah, one to Asaph, and one to Solomon. Four others are anonymous. Book Two's doxology is found in Ps. 72:18–20:

> Praise be to the LORD God, the God of Israel, who alone does marvelous deeds. Praise be to his glorious name forever; may the whole earth be filled with his glory. Amen and Amen. (NIV)

Hymnbook Three: Psalms 73–89

Considered the "Psalms of David's Singers" by some scholars, these psalms contain eleven credited to Asaph, one credited to David, one credited to Ethan, and four to the sons of Korah. They emphasize the Lord as Elohim and Jehovah as the mighty helper, and they encourage people to ceaselessly worship Him. Concluding Book Three is Ps. 89:52:

> Praise be to the LORD forever! Amen and Amen. (NIV)

Hymnbook Four: Psalms 90–106

Most likely compiled after Israel's captivity, these psalms focus on Jehovah's victory and reign, and on the restoration of Israel. Moses is credited with one of them, David with two, and the remainder are anonymous. God is praised as Jehovah, the governing king; the name Jehovah is used 126 times. This and the following book originally formed one collection. Book Four concludes with Ps. 106:48:

> Praise be to the LORD, the God of Israel, from everlasting to everlasting. Let all the people say, 'Amen!' Praise the LORD. (NIV)

Hymnbook Five: Psalms 107–150

Called the "Songs of Degrees," these psalms were sung after Israel's captivity and relate to the ascent of God's people as they traveled from the wilderness up to Jerusalem. In them, they depend upon and jubilantly praise their beloved with hallelujahs. David is credited with 15 of these psalms, Solomon with one, and 28 are anonymous. This final songbook emphasizes God as Jehovah, the Redeemer, who deserves to be worshiped by the redeemed.

While the entire text of Ps. 150 may have served as the doxology for the Psalter as a whole, Ps. 150:6 probably functioned as the conclusion for this book:

> Let everything that has breath praise the LORD. Praise the LORD. (NIV)

Classification of the Psalms

Use and Theme

In their attempts to study Psalms, scholars have classified the Psalter according to the psalms' uses, their thematic motifs, and their content. Just as today we sing particular hymns during certain seasons—resurrection hymns at Easter, for example—the ancient Hebrews also sang seasonal psalms. Based on the title provided for Pss. 120–134, "Song of Ascents," it appears that pilgrims sang these psalms while going up to Jerusalem to celebrate Passover, Tabernacles and Pentecost.

Psalms have been grouped as:

- Praise hymns (Pss. 8, 19, 29, 65, 96)

- Hymns of personal and national crises (Pss. 3, 35, 43, 44, 60, 63, 80, 86, 123)

- Faith songs of personal thanksgiving (Pss. 18, 32, 40, 118, 144)

- Prayers of communion (Pss. 11, 17, 23, 36, 103, 116, 138)

- Meditations of wisdom (Pss. 1, 12, 37, 90, 111, 119, 127)

- Royal hymns (Pss. 1, 2, 20, 45, 72, 110)

- Prophetic oracles (Pss. 81, 82)

Other themes include:

- Victory, lamentation, the coming king (Pss. 93–100)

- God's attributes and character, penitence, hallelujah-praise (Pss. 146–150)

Sabbath liturgies as in Ps. 68:24–25 that reveal a specific procession sional use:

Your procession has come into view, O God, the procession of my God and King into the sanctuary. In front are the singers, after them the musicians; with them are the maidens playing tambourines. (NIV)

Over time individual psalms became part of standardized liturgies that the Hebrews recited or sang to offer thanksgiving, to express praise, and to make petition and supplication when facing serious illness or injustice. The Israelites either chanted themselves or requested others to sing the appropriate psalm(s) for them in the temple. This frequent repetition as part of worship aided in the preservation of the psalms across the centuries.

Historical Occasions or Events

Unlike most modern songs, however, each psalm included in the Psalter may have been linked to a specific historical occasion or event.

Consider the following psalms and the Scriptures with which they are associated:

Psalm	Historic Event	Related Scriptures
16	Delivery of Nathan's Promise to David	1 Chr. 17, 2 Sam. 7
30	Dedication of Araunah's Threshing Floor	1 Chr. 21
42	David's Flight from Absalom	2 Sam. 15–17
54	Treachery of the Ziphites	1 Sam. 23
84	Founding of the Second Temple	Ezra 3
92	Babylonian Captivity	Dan. 7
142	David's Stay in the Cave of Adullam	1 Sam. 22

Psalms and Associated Scriptures
Figure 8.1

Psalms Put to Music

I will sing a new song to you, O God; on the ten-stringed lyre I will make music to you, to the One who gives victory to kings, who delivers his servant David from the deadly sword. —Psalm 144:9–10 (NIV)

The poetry of the Psalms, like other poetry, has patterns of meter, the rhythm of successive syllables. Because of the psalms' importance and the stressed syllables found in them, the texts of various psalms were used in psalmodic chanting or recitative-style musical performance during temple worship in Jerusalem.

To some people, the Psalter was instructive because the chanted texts taught correct separation of phrases and words. Sometimes a singer would sing the melody of a verse and others would answer by repeating some of it. A soloist could alternate with singers or combine with them to sing refrains together. Typically, within the temple, the temple choir sang on the peoples' behalf.

Some psalms were written to be antiphonal, sung by two or more groups. Ps. 24, for example, was no doubt sung by two choirs, the recurring phrases facilitating response to previous verses.

During the first centuries, believers recognized the power inherent within the hymns of the Psalter. Psalmody, a practice by which a text was reproduced tonally in repeated, advanced patterns, formed the foundation upon which church music was based. In fact, the power of psalmody was credited with focusing believers' minds on godly things, generating good conduct and even transmitting a mystic service to God.

Compared to today's hymns, the music of the ancient Hebrews was contemplative, symbolic, and steeped in ritual. The Psalms incorporated many features of music and poetry. Imagine the glorious sounds as the Levitical singers, appointed musicians of the sanctuary, made offerings of song while meat, grain, and drink offerings were being sacrificed.

Preservation of the Psalter

Gradually collected over a period of nearly six centuries, the 150 individual psalms testify to God's preservation of His inspired Word. These psalms reflect the deep desire and honest struggle of the ancient psalmists to reach out to God, to experience His divine presence, to touch the ultimate source of all life. Thus, we not only learn about the writers themselves from the psalms, we learn God-inspired truths that continue to be meaningful and relevant to our lives today.

The book of Psalms remains as vibrant and important to faith, doctrine, and worship as it was during the time of the ancient Hebrews. It is nothing short of miraculous that the psalms survived for centuries, especially when we consider the high percentage of ancient Greek literary works that did not survive the ravages of time. What enabled the Psalter to survive time, nature, and historical upheavals while more recent Greek works were lost? Only God knows.

Musical Instruments of the Psalter

By reading the superscriptions or introductions to each psalm, we gain valuable insight into the instruments that accompanied it. For example, the superscription to Ps. 5 reads, "For the director of music. For flutes." Psalm 55 was to be performed "with stringed instruments." Many psalms are described as "a psalm," which probably referred to those that were performed to the accompaniment of a plucked stringed instrument. (For a list of references to Bible instruments, see Appendix D.)

A number of psalms mention instruments within the poetry. Consider the following:

- Praise the LORD with the harp; make music to him on the ten-stringed lyre. (Psalm 33:2 NIV)

- I will sing and make music. Awake, my soul! Awake, harp and lyre! I will awaken the dawn. (Psalm 57:7–8 NIV)

- Begin the music, strike the tambourine, play the melodious harp and lyre. Sound the ram's horn at the New Moon. (Psalm 81:2–3 NIV)

- It is good to praise the LORD and make music to your name, O Most High, to proclaim your love in the morning and your faithfulness at night, to the music of the ten-stringed lyre and the melody of the harp. (Psalm 92:1–3 NIV)

- Praise him with the sounding of the trumpet, praise him with the harp and lyre, praise him with tambourine and dancing, praise him with the strings and flute, praise him with the clash of cymbals. (Psalm 150:3–5 NIV)

It appears that some introductions to the Psalms actually explained the melodic tunes to be played or the mode of performance to be used. For example, Ps. 57 reads, "For the director of music. To the tune of 'Do Not Destroy'" (NIV). Nevertheless we know little about the actual sound of the psalmic music, although old liturgical chants seem to relate to Yemenite Jewish music which in turn appears to have changed little since biblical times.

Some scholars believe that the word *Selah*, which appears 71 times in 39 psalms, indicates an instrumental interlude or a point where people could join their voices to the instrumental accompaniment. (For a list of psalms that mention song or singing, see Appendix A.)

The Joy of Studying the Psalms

Whether as an academic, a novice poet, or a layperson, we have in the Psalms an incredible opportunity to connect with Christians throughout the centuries. Reading the Psalms provides us with a platform from which we can praise our Creator. Throughout the coming year, read your way through the Psalms and experience the incredible blessing that comes from reading poetry. If you like, try setting a short Psalm to music. Listen to the melody and cadence that reading the Psalm aloud makes. Just try it. The discipline of doing so may break open the doors and allow you to enter into a deeper communion with the Lord of All.

9

Songs of Isaiah

Burst into songs of joy together. —Isaiah 52:9 (NIV)

THE POETRY, VISION, AND IMPACT of the prophet Isaiah are unsurpassed in the Holy Scriptures. Old Testament scholars have long recognized this prophet as a man of long-lived influence. The book bearing his name is made up of sixty-six chapters and is a miniature Bible with its sixty-six books. We know that Isaiah was a well-known public figure, was highly educated, and moved freely among royalty and nobility. He may well have come from the aristocracy in Jerusalem, his home and the scene of his labors. Isaiah was a family man: his wife was a prophetess (Isa. 8:3) and bore two sons, both of whose names were symbolic of the themes Isaiah emphasized in his prophecies. To confirm that Isaiah was held in high regard both during his lifetime and in the years to follow, we need only turn to words from Ben Sira's eulogy in the early second century B.C., "a great man trustworthy in his vision. . . . In the power of the spirit he saw the last things . . . he revealed the future to the end of time, and hidden things long before they happened."[1]

Isaiah was confident, a man of courage and unafraid to confront kings; though he spoke harsh words of judgment reviling the iniquity and sinfulness of the people, Isaiah spoke poignantly and compassionately of comfort, hope, and promise for the future.

Orator

Isaiah spoke a message of deliberate consistency with three primary themes:

- God is King of heaven and earth, the Holy One of Israel, righteous and everlasting.

- The people of God have fallen into iniquity, and salvation will come only through total and complete dependence on Yahweh.

- While kings on the throne of David may come and go, the Everlasting King is the security upon whom the nation of Israel will be assured. (6:1–4)

Isaiah, a name coming from the Hebrew meaning "salvation of God" or "God is salvation," was a prophet intent on drawing his nation back to righteousness. He most assuredly delivered his messages orally; and his words were often repeated and widely disseminated. Perhaps it is for this reason the words of Isaiah have the greatest impact today when we hear them proclaimed from the pulpit or rendered with orchestral power and majesty in the classic work, *The Messiah*, by George Frideric Handel (1741).

This articulate, eloquent orator stands in a long line of prophets, from those who spoke with the brevity of Obadiah (21 verses) to Jeremiah (with 1,364). Yet Isaiah stands alone in the remarkable accuracy of its preservation from the oldest known scrolls and manuscripts, an undisputable fact indicating that all 1,290 verses which make up his many oracles, messages, and narratives were long recognized in the early church as sacred texts, a veritable treasury of prophecy, wisdom, and righteous admonition for those who fear the Lord!

Poet

No other Old Testament writer used so many beautiful and picturesque illustrations, epigrams, and metaphors as Isaiah, a poet of extraordinary skill. One has only to close one's eyes and imagine the lone tenor voice in the opening lines of Handel's *Messiah* be lifted by the poetic mastery of Isa. 40:1–3 (KJV):

Comfort ye, comfort ye my people, saith your God.

Speak ye comfortably to Jerusalem, and cry unto her, that her warfare is accomplished, that her iniquity is pardoned. . . .

The voice of him that crieth in the wilderness:
Prepare ye the way of the LORD, make straight in the desert a highway for our God.

Statesman

Isaiah was an ardent patriot, loving God and his nation. He was bold and truthful, seeking no court favor, strongly denouncing all foreign alliances (Isa. 7:5; 37:22), confident that future of the the nation of Israel was to be found in the righteousness of Yahweh. Isaiah's message was clear: deliverance would come from dependence on Yahweh alone! In Isa. 2:2, 4 (NRSV), it is this prophet who gave us the earliest recorded vision of worldwide peace:

In days to come the mountain of the LORD's house shall be established as the highest of the mountains,
and shall be raised above the hills;
all the nations shall stream to it.

He shall judge between the nations,
and shall arbitrate for many peoples;
they shall beat their swords into plowshares,
and their spears into pruning hooks;
nation shall not lift up sword against nation,
neither shall they learn war any more.

Reformer

Like Moses, Samuel, and others who came before him, Isaiah was a preacher of righteousness. He railed against legalism and rote performance of ritual and sacrifice as a bad substitute for the truly spiritual life and conduct. Yet, amid all his rebukes and denunciations of evil, Isaiah was truly optimistic, like all the greatest contributors to moral uplift.

They will enter Zion with singing;
everlasting joy will crown their heads.
Gladness and joy will overtake them,
and sorrow and sighing will flee away.
(Isa. 35:10 NIV)

Prophet

In no uncertain language, Isaiah foretold the future of Israel and Judah and the downfall of Gentile nations.

The people walking in darkness have seen a great light. . . .
For to us a child is born, to us a son is given,
    and the government will be on his shoulders.
And he will be called
Wonderful Counselor, Mighty God, Everlasting Father, Prince of
    Peace.
(Isa. 9:2, 6 NIV)

By the Word of God, which is the sword of the Spirit, the prophecy foretelling the coming of the Messiah came to pass in Bethlehem indeed. The divine work foretold in many of Isaiah's predictions regarding ancient nations has been fulfilled, but the fulfillment of God's work within and through the world is a study for another time.

Musician

Isaiah could hear the mountains sing and the fields shout for joy, for the Lord was his strength and song. He was a man attuned not only to the voice of God, but also to the cries of his people who were in bondage. The prophet gave them songs of hope and praise. At times he proclaimed God's displeasure with some of the other musical sounds heard in the streets of Zion:

The LORD says,
"The women of Zion are haughty,
walking along with outstretched necks,

flirting with their eyes,
tripping along with mincing steps,
with ornaments jingling on their ankles."
(Isa. 3:16 NIV)

The following twelve songs reference almost every walk of life and show forth the splendour and majesty of God's creation.

- For the one I love a song about his vineyard. (Isa. 5:1)

- The LORD, is my strength and my song. (Isa.12:2)

- To Tyre as in the song of the prostitute. (Isa.23:15)

- Play the harp well, sing many a song. (Isa.23:16)

- No longer do they drink wine with a song. (Isa. 24:9)

- So the song of the ruthless is stilled. (Isa. 25:5)

- In that day this song will be sung in the land. (Isa. 26:1)

- Sing to the LORD a new song. (Isa. 42:10)

- Burst into song, O mountains! (Isa. 49:13)

- Burst into song, shout for joy, you who were never in labor. (Isa. 54:1)

- The mountains and hills will burst into song. (Isa. 55:12)

Selected Songs of Isaiah

The Song of the Vineyard

Isa. 5:1–7

The first seven verses of Isa. 5 may be read as a love song of God's tender care for his people, a parable of an unholy nation, and an oracle. Beginning with the opening lines, the prophet clearly identifies the words to come as a "song," a song of judgment foreshadowing a time when Israel "shall have a song / As in the night when a holy festival is kept, / And gladness of heart as when one goes with a flute, / To come into the mountain of the LORD, / To the Mighty One of Israel" (30:29 NKJV). Isaiah is speaking to his people as with the heart of God.

Now will I sing to my wellbeloved
a song of my beloved touching his vineyard.
(Isa. 5:1 KJV)

The "Song of the Vineyard," which should be read along with the "Parable of the Vineyard" (Matt. 21:33–44), moves quickly from God's wonderful love for man to man's rebellion against, and rejection of, such amazing love.

My wellbeloved hath a vineyard
in a very fruitful hill:

And he fenced it,
and gathered out the stones thereof,
and planted it with the choicest vine,
and built a tower in the midst of it,
and also made a winepress therein:
and he looked that it should bring forth grapes,
and it brought forth wild grapes.

And now, O inhabitants of Jerusalem, and men of Judah,
judge, I pray you, betwixt me and my vineyard.

What could have been done more to my vineyard,
that I have not done in it?
wherefore, when I looked that it should bring forth grapes,
brought it forth wild grapes?

And now go to;
I will tell you what I will do to my vineyard:
I will take away the hedge thereof,
and it shall be eaten up;
and break down the wall thereof,
and it shall be trodden down:

And I will lay it waste:
it shall not be pruned, nor digged;
but there shall come up briers and thorns:

I will also command the clouds
that they rain no rain upon it.

For the vineyard of the LORD of hosts
is the house of Israel,
and the men of Judah
his pleasant plant:
and he looked for judgment, but behold oppression;
for righteousness, but behold a cry.
(Isa. 5:1–7 KJV)

Israel's tragedy is our own. God seeks to make our lives fruitful vineyards. Alas, some produce "briers and thorns" instead of luscious grapes, a phrase found nowhere else in the Old Testament except in Isaiah. Interesting to note that Isaiah uses this phrase again and again to describe what follows the harsh judgment of the Holy One!

Israel, however, as God's true vineyard, will gloriously flourish so that the whole earth shall be filled with fruit. Dealing with these divine chastisements, Isaiah makes it plain that Israel's judgment will be light compared with God's judgment of surrounding godless nations. Though the judgment of the nations was, and will be, punitive, God's judgment of the beloved people of Israel is always remedial. God sifts the chaff and destroys the nations, but what comfort we can take from the declaration, "For the people shall dwell in Zion. . . . You shall weep no more. He will be very gracious to you at the sound of your cry." (Isa. 30:19 NKJV). Burdened soul, ever remember that God will never allow you to carry more than you are able to bear.

A Song of Thanksgiving

Isa. 12:1–6
Concluding the first major section of Isaiah (1–12), this is a hymn of praise for the great mercies promised to the children of Israel. It is not only the shortest chapter in Isaiah, but one of the sweetest, celebrating Israel's deliverance from the Babylonian captivity and their redemption by the Messiah, and it emphasizes the future and the hope for Israel.

The chapter appears to be in two halves. In the first two verses, a personal note is prominent with the use of "I" and "my." Speaking with first person pronouns clearly tells us that any saint can lay hold of the Lord as the prophet describes. We can without doubt or fear make the majesty and mystery of God "my salvation," "my strength," and "my song" (v. 2).

> And in that day thou shalt say,
> O LORD, I will praise thee:
> though thou wast angry with me,
> thine anger is turned away,
> and thou comfortedst me.
>
> Behold, God is my salvation;
> I will trust, and not be afraid:
> for the LORD JEHOVAH is my strength and my song;
> he also is become my salvation.
> (Isa. 12:1–2 KJV)

Note the repetition of the phrase "in that day" (vv. 1, 4). These are fearful days, and many are afraid. This chapter offers people in the world, and a world of people, a cure for despair (v. 2). Faith and fear can never exist together. The one expels the other. The Holy One in our midst is our salvation. If He is our salvation, He will be our strength. And as we appropriate Him as our strength, we come to know Him as our song.

The second half of the chapter is an edict for the people of God. Describing the worship of the millennial host, the prophet proclaims that those forming the kingdom are to be a singing people. As for the many "wells of salvation" from which we can draw refreshing water (v. 3), what joy they produce!

> Therefore with joy shall ye draw water
> out of the wells of salvation.
>
> And in that day shall ye say,
> Praise the LORD, call upon his name,
> declare his doings among the people,
> make mention that his name is exalted.

Sing unto the LORD; for he hath done excellent things:
this is known in all the earth.

Cry out and shout, thou inhabitant of Zion:
for great is the Holy One of Israel in the midst of thee.
(Isa. 12:3–6, KJV)

Song of Judah's Return

Isa. 26
The first six verses of Isa. 26, much like Chapter 25, are a song of
victory and praise followed by verses 7–21, a hymn of lament and reassurance. Thanksgivings for temporal and spiritual mercies are beautifully mingled, though the latter still predominates throughout the
song and hymn. Even the sublime and evangelical doctrine of the resurrection seems to be hinted at in verse 19 (NRSV):

Your dead shall live, their corpses shall rise.
O dwellers in the dust, awake and sing for joy!

Typifying the deliverance of the people of God from captivity and
misery, this song and subsequent hymn are beautifully diversified by
the frequent changes of speakers. It opens with a chorus of the church
celebrating the protection vouchsafed by God to His people. The happiness of the righteous, whom He guards, is contrasted with the misery
of the wicked, whom He punishes.

In that day shall this song be sung in the land of Judah;
We have a strong city;
salvation will God appoint
for walls and bulwarks.

Open ye the gates,
that the righteous nation which keepeth the truth may enter in.

Thou wilt keep him in perfect peace,
whose mind is stayed on thee:
because he trusteth in thee.

Trust ye in the LORD for ever:
for in the LORD JEHOVAH is everlasting strength:

For he bringeth down them that dwell on high;
the lofty city, he layeth it low;
he layeth it low, even to the ground;
he bringeth it even to the dust.

The foot shall tread it down,
even the feet of the poor,
and the steps of the needy.

The way of the just is uprightness:
thou, most upright, dost weigh the path of the just.
(Isa. 26:1–7 KJV)

Here the prophet breaks in, speaking in his own voice, eagerly catching the last words of the chorus (vv. 8–9), which were perfectly in unison with the feelings of his own soul and which he beautifully repeats, as one musical instrument reverberates the sound of another on the same key.

Yea, in the way of thy judgments, O LORD,
have we waited for thee;
the desire of our soul is to thy name,
and to the remembrance of thee.

With my soul have I desired thee in the night;
yea, with my spirit within me will I seek thee early:
for when thy judgments are in the earth,
the inhabitants of the world will learn righteousness.
(Isa. 26:8–9 KJV)

Chapter 26 moves flowingly from a song of praise to a hymn of lament and comes back again with reassurance that the prayers of Israel will be answered and the Lord's judgment will be just. Taken together, this is a bold proclamation of hope and a proclamation of the coming restoration of the nation of Israel. Is it any wonder that with a message of such enduring promise, salvation, and redemption, the language in which these words were first spoken has a surprisingly large vocabulary for music! Indeed, Old Testament scholars have long known that "the terms for vocal music outnumber by far the purely instrumental ones."

The Song of the Redeemed

Isa. 35:1–10

Joy after judgment! Song after storm! The crashing finale of divine judgment in Isa. 34 is followed by the sweetest strains of promise in the "Song of the Redeemed" in 35:1–10. Death and darkness depart, and the very desert "laughs with abundance." Delight is everywhere. F. C. Jennings writes:

> The very storm affords a foil that increases the sweetness of that calm. Little do they know of the delights of springs who have never felt the pinch of winter; little do they value the 'time of the singing of birds' who have never lacked their melody; little should we care for the promise, "God shall wipe away all tears," had we never wept. So this lovely little chapter is doubly refreshing from its sharp contrast with its predecessor. It has a lilt of joy and is almost metrical in our Authorized Version without much change.[2]

Much of the imagery of this chapter seems to be borrowed from the exodus from Egypt, but the life, sentiments, and passions ascribed to inanimate objects enliven the retelling. For beauty of expression, the language of Isa. 35 is peerless. The reality of blessedness described goes well beyond the glowing terms used. All nature rejoices with the people of God for their deliverance, relief, and comfort, giving some commentators cause to think this song is a prophecy referring to heaven. A verse like the eighth, however, is one to be realized in the present lives of the redeemed.

> The wilderness and the solitary place shall be glad for them;
> and the desert shall rejoice, and blossom as the rose.

> It shall blossom abundantly,
> and rejoice even with joy and singing:
> the glory of Lebanon shall be given unto it,
> the excellency of Carmel and Sharon,
> they shall see the glory of the LORD,
> and the excellency of our God.

Strengthen ye the weak hands,
and confirm the feeble knees.

Say to them that are of a fearful heart,
Be strong, fear not:
behold, your God will come with vengeance,
even God with a recompence;
he will come and save you.

Then the eyes of the blind shall be opened,
and the ears of the deaf shall be unstopped.

Then shall the lame man leap as an hart,
and the tongue of the dumb sing:
for in the wilderness shall waters break out,
and streams in the desert.

And the parched ground shall become a pool,
and the thirsty land springs of water:
in the habitation of dragons, where each lay,
shall be grass with reeds and rushes.

And an highway shall be there, and a way,
and it shall be called The way of holiness;
the unclean shall not pass over it;
but it shall be for those:
the wayfaring men, though fools, shall not err therein.

No lion shall be there,
nor any ravenous beast shall go up thereon,
it shall not be found there;
but the redeemed shall walk there:

And the ransomed of the LORD shall return,
and come to Zion with songs and everlasting joy upon their heads:
they shall obtain joy and gladness,
and sorrow and sighing shall flee away.
(Isa. 35:1–10 KJV)

One cannot help but see the inclusion of *all* of creation in this song,
for indeed, all of creation, from the simple bloom of a crocus to the

leaping of the lame, all of the ransomed ones shall be on the highway of the Holy Way. These are words of the transforming work of God in the world: the weak hands made strong; the feeble made firm; the fearful made fearless. True yesterday, today and forever, the Word of the Lord proclaims the promise of new life!

Old Testament scholar Walter Brueggeman asserts:

Our reading of this text must not tone down or apologize for its lyrical abandonment. The poem is a healing alternative to the church's grim despair and to our modern sense that no real newness is possible.[3]

Song for King Hezekiah's Recovery

Isa. 38:9–20

In the fourteenth year of King Hezekiah's reign, when he was about thirty-eight years of age, Isaiah was divinely commanded to pronounce the king's death, going to the King and saying, "Set thine house in order; for thou shalt die and not live" (v. 1 KJV).

This song in verses 9–20 is an account of King Hezekiah's dangerous sickness and miraculous recovery. Since the king had no son at the time, Messianic hopes that were centered in the dynasty of David were seriously threatened. Hezekiah prayed earnestly and his death sentence was revoked. God added fifteen years to his life, in which time a son was born.

The poetic song of thanksgiving in Isa. 38:9–20 fittingly expresses the sentiments and feelings of one who was unexpectedly and miraculously delivered from the brink of death. The king's hopeless melancholy gives way to boundless rapture as he learns of continued life in communion with God in the land of the living.

I said, I shall not see the LORD
in the land of the living;
I shall look upon mortals no more. . . .

I cry for help until morning;

My eyes are weary with looking upward.
(Isa 38:11–14 NRSV)

We must remember, as we read of Hezekiah's gloomy view of the future, that he did not have the clear revelation of the New Testament. It was our Lord Jesus who brought life and immortality to light through His gospel (2 Tim. 1:10), and so this ode may be adapted to other cases and will always afford profit and pleasure to those who are not void of feeling and piety.

> Surely it was for my welfare
> that I had great bitterness;
> but you have held back my life
> from the pit of destruction,
> for you have cast all my sins
> behind your back.
> (Isa 38:17 NRSV)

> The Lord was ready to save me;
> Therefore we will sing my songs with stringed instruments
> All the days of our life,
> In the house of the LORD.
> (Isa. 38:20 NKJV)

A Harper and Singers[4]
Figure 9.1

Song of Comfort for God's People

Isa. 40:1–31

With this final song to which we now turn our attention, we come to the second half of Isaiah. Martin Luther said Isaiah divides easily into "two books": the first part is comprised of historical narratives in roughly chronological order interspersed with sections of poetic verse and song; the second part is that of prophetic poetry without any historical narratives. Calvin and his predecessors clearly noticed the differences in "literary style, content and vocabulary."

In chapters 1 to 39, Isaiah looked toward the captivity. In chapters 40–66, he looks beyond captivity toward the future hope of a restored nation. The two opening verses of this chapter provide a prologue for the entire second half of Isaiah. The basis of Israel's comfort is the infinite, all wise, all-powerful God, who in comparison with other gods is incomparable. Such is the undisputable sovereignty of the God of Abraham, Isaac and Jacob!

> Comfort ye, comfort ye my people,
> saith your God.

> Speak ye comfortably to Jerusalem,
> and cry unto her,
> that her warfare is accomplished,
> that her iniquity is pardoned:
> for she hath received of the LORD's hand
> double for all her sins.
> (Isa. 40:1–2 KJV)

Though scholarship shows us that First Isaiah never existed apart or independently from Second Isaiah, neither was intended to be a "history" book, but divinely inspired Scripture with a spiritual purpose much greater than a simple recounting of historical events. Despite the differences between what is often called "First Isaiah" and "Second Isaiah," this prophetic masterpiece of history and prophecy is unquestionably the Word of God as given through a human servant, prophet of the Holy One, a favorite term of the prophet Isaiah.

In this song of comfort, the prophet considers the restoration of God's people with great force and elegance. Isaiah declares God's command to His messengers to comfort His people in their captivity and to impart to them the glad tidings that the time of favor and deliverance is at hand (vv. 1–2).

Immediately a harbinger is introduced, giving orders to remove every obstacle and to prepare the way for their return to their own land.

> The voice of him that crieth in the wilderness,
> Prepare ye the way of the LORD,
> make straight in the desert a highway for our God.
>
> Every valley shall be exalted,
> and every mountain and hill shall be made low:
> and the crooked shall be made straight,
> and the rough places plain:
>
> And the glory of the LORD shall be revealed,
> and all flesh shall see it together:
> for the mouth of the LORD hath spoken it.
> (Isa. 40:3–5 KJV)

These same words appear in the New Testament, calling believers to enter into the path of the good news (Matt. 3:3; John 1:23). All attention is turned from temporary, fading things to spiritual and eternal things (Isa. 40:6–11).

The power and wisdom of God, the Creator of Heaven and Earth, will remove every obstacle in the way of both the return of Israel and the entrance of believers into His kingdom. The contrast between the great Jehovah and everything reputed to be great in this world strikes the listener with inexpressible reverence and self-abasement (vv. 12–26). The prophet concludes with a comfortable application by showing that God's infinite power and unsearchable wisdom is everlastingly given to strengthening, comforting, and saving His people (vv. 27–31).

If it is not an exaggeration to say that the Hebrew word ḥesed, translated as "unfailing love" or "steadfast love" is the undeniable message of the Psalms, as some scholars claim, then it is no less true that the message of Isaiah is to heed the holiness of God and take comfort in God's power and might. What more could give us reason to sing God's praise?

10

King Solomon's Song of Songs

Flowers appear on the earth; the season of singing has come, the cooing of doves is heard in our land. —Song of Solomon 2:12 (NIV)

THINK OF THE ADVANTAGES with which Solomon began his career. He claimed almost undisputed possession of David's throne. Immense stores of wealth were laid up for him by his father. He possessed exceptional, divinely-imparted mental abilities. Finally, his people loved him and had high hopes for his reign. Solomon's start, like the cloudless dawn of a summer's morning, might have continued all his life, but it ended in gloom. The man who penned and preached a thousand wise things failed to practice the wisdom he taught. A life beginning magnificently ended miserably. Yet despite his failures, Solomon's song of love continues to be celebrated today.

Solomon's Most Beautiful Song

The Hebrew Bible calls this song the Song of Songs or Canticles (Latin translation), possibly indicating that Solomon considered it the choicest of all the 1,005 songs that he wrote (1 Kgs. 4:32). A love song set in blossoming springtime, the poem abounds in metaphor and reads with a profusion of oriental imagery and exhibits Solomon's fondness for nature, gardens, meadows, vineyards, orchards, and flocks (1 Kgs. 4:33). Tradition claims it was written to celebrate his marriage to his favorite wife, but whatever the occasion or inspiration of this music, the

Song of Solomon certainly celebrates love in a manner unique among the books of the Bible.

Poetry

Biblical scholarship offers little definitive research when it comes to this sublime work. Some scholars think the "Song of Songs" was originally 31 poems now fused into one poetic work; others believe this love song is one unified poem, written with a tightly constructed, intricate pattern. Yet all scholars familiar with the structure of Hebrew poetry consider this poem to be a superb composition. The Song of Songs contains several different types of poetry in the song including a specific type of poetic passage (a *wasf*) not found anywhere else in the Bible. Some of the poetic lines may easily be viewed as actual song lyrics, an opinion because they are "brief, sensual, musical in which intensely subjective experience is recorded."[1] Nonetheless, though it is thought to be one of the most beautiful examples of Hebrew poetry in the Old Testament, its sudden transitions from speaker to speaker and place to place, with no explanation of shifting scenes and actors, make this book difficult to follow and understand. In Hebrew, the change of speakers is indicated by gender; in many English Bibles, by extra space.

Lover
How beautiful you are, my darling!
Oh, how beautiful!
Your eyes are doves.

Beloved
How handsome you are, my lover!
Oh, how charming!
And our bed is verdant.
(Song 1:15–16 NIV)

Author and Singers

Tradition suggests that Solomon probably wrote this book while he was a young man, although modern scholarship has brought that dating into question. Nonetheless, we can clearly determine that the singers are a bride, called the Shulammite (6:13), the king, and a chorus of palace ladies called "daughters of Jerusalem." Solomon's harem was as yet small, only sixty wives and eighty concubines with innumerable maidens on the waiting list (6:8). Eventually it grew to include seven hundred wives and three hundred concubines (1 Kgs. 11:3). A common opinion, and probably the best, is that the Shulammite was Abishag of Shunem, the fairest maiden in all the land, who attended David in his last days (1 Kgs. 1:1–4).

> They searched throughout Israel for a beautiful girl and found Abishag. . . . The girl was very beautiful; she took care of the king and waited on him. (1 Kgs. 1:3–4 NIV)

She, no doubt, became Solomon's wife, for her marriage to another might have endangered his throne (1 Kings 2:17, 22).

Interpretations

Probably no book of the Bible has been interpreted in as many different ways as the Song of Solomon. These interpretations typically fall into two categories: literal and allegorical.

Theodore of Mopsuestia (fourth century A.D.) believes it is a straightforward poem that Solomon wrote in honor of his marriage. Johann David Michaelis suggests the book simply expresses God's approval of marriage, while J. F. W. Bousset supposes that it was a poetic marriage drama used in ancient times as part of the wedding rituals, though no dramatic structure exists within the text such as acts, scenes, or narrator(s). The modern scholar Calvin Seerveld sees it as an ancient love story with a strong religious and spiritual message. A simple reading of the text can easily be interpreted as a eulogy of the joys of wedded life, its essence found in its tender and devoted expressions of the intimate delights of wedded love. Even if this poem is no more than that, it is worthy of a place in God's word because marriage was ordained of God (Gen. 2:24). Proper mutual attitudes in the inner familiarities of married life contribute, in no small measure, to human happiness and well-being.

However, both Jews and Christians have seen deeper meanings in this song for centuries. Consider the following line, often sung in Christian worship services today:

> He has taken me to the banquet hall, and his banner over me is love. (Song 2:4 NIV)

The Jewish Talmud teaches that the book is an allegory of God's love for Israel, and indeed Israel is often called God's wife in the Old Testament (Jer. 3:1; Ezek. 16; 23). Jews read it at Passover as an allegorical reference to the Exodus, when God espoused Israel to Himself as His bride. His love for Israel is exemplified here as the spontaneous love of a great king and a humble maid. Christians quite commonly regard it as the prenuptial song of Christ and the church. In the New Testament Jesus is called a bridegroom (Matt. 9:15; 25:1; John 3:29), and the church is called the bride of Christ (2 Cor. 11:2; Eph. 5:23; Rev. 21:2; 22:17), indicating that human wedlock is a sort of counterpart and foretaste of the rapturous relation between Christ and the church.

How a man with a thousand women could love any one of them in a manner fitting to be typical of Christ's love for the church is difficult to imagine. However Solomon lived in a time and place in which polygamy was commonly practiced and an accepted cultural norm. A number of Old Testament saints were, indeed, polygamists. In Old Testament times the saints practiced prevailing customs, and Scripture depicts such with honesty. Kings generally took many wives as a sign of royalty, power, wealth, and good diplomacy. Solomon's devotion to this lovely girl did seem to be genuine and unmistakable. Then, too, he was king in the family that produced the Messiah, and it seems not unfitting that his marriage should, in a sense, prefigure the Messiah's eternal marriage to His bride. The joys of this song, we think, will find their climax in the hallelujahs of the Lamb's marriage supper (Rev. 19:6–9).

Song of Songs

Throughout the centuries there are those who questioned the inclusion of this ancient Hebrew poem in the sacred canon; however, the

Jews thought of it as the "holy of holies of Scripture." Christians have traditionally accepted the dialogue between bridegroom and bride as that which typifies the mystery of Christ and His church. (Ps. 45; Isa. 62:5), yet that interpretation fails to adequately acknowledge the explicit references to human love and the fact that the name of God is never specifically mentioned in the text. Is it not possible that in the mystery and magnificence of Holy God of Israel, both interpretations are valid and hold merit for followers of Christ willing to delve into the riches of this Holy text? The Scriptures present us with a remarkable array of texts, narratives, stories, and parables all intended to reveal the true, everlasting, and unchanging character of God. Whether read as a spiritual allegory detailing the unfailing pursuit of God for his people, or read as describing the sacrament of marriage and the sanctity of human love and devotion, this poem allows *both,* in fact, to tell us something about our Lord and Giver of life.

> Many waters cannot quench love,
> Nor can the floods drown it.
> If a man would give for love
> All the wealth of his house,
> It would be utterly despised.
> (Song 8:7 NKJV)

PART 3

■ ■ ■

The Universal Church Sings

11

Songs of the New Testament

The meaning of song goes deep. Who is there that, in logical words, can express the effect music has on us? A kind of inarticulate, unfathomable speech, which leads us to the edge of the infinite, and lets us for moments gaze into that!
—Thomas Carlyle

FROM THE CLOSING WORDS of the Old Testament to the coming of the new covenant in Jesus Christ, hundreds of years passed. In those years between the old and new covenants, The Lord God Almighty seemed to grow silent: no more burning bushes or parting waters; no more angelic messengers. The people of God were waiting for the promised Messiah, waiting for God to once again act mightily. Into this period of waiting came the angel Gabriel announcing a child was to be born. Into this time of waiting came a decree from Caesar Augustus. Into this time of waiting, God's presence was once again made manifest.

Early Christians stood at a momentous intersection of God's divine work in history, witnessing remarkable events that forever changed the course of human history. Living during the time when Jesus walked on the earth, they witnessed the miraculous events surrounding our Savior's birth; they witnessed the loving kindness and mighty power of God Incarnate in the life and death of Jesus Christ. These early believers were vessels of inspiration, instruction, and indeed, walked through the very crucible of the formation of the Church. As we turn from our study of music in the Old Testament to the New, the Gospel of Luke becomes the first book of the New Testament to which we turn. The only gospel written by a disciple who did not walk alongside Jesus as one of the chosen twelve,

Luke's gospel is distinctive in several respects that are pertinent to our purposes here.

First, Luke is the only gospel that continues with a sequel: the "orderly account" (Luke 1:3 NRSV) Luke sets out to write to Theophilus and continues with the Book of Acts, making Luke-Acts the largest volume of writing by a single contributor to the New Testament. Of the four gospels, Luke is most attentive to thorough research, to an accurate, chronological telling of the events of Jesus' life. Some scholars and historians have called Luke the "theological historian," because of his frequent mention of specific historical places, people, and events.

But perhaps most distinct of all is the detailed description Luke gives to the beginning and end of Jesus' life on earth. Luke's contribution includes the unique telling of the story of Jesus birth. In fact, fully twenty-five percent of the Gospel of Luke is not found in any other gospel, and most of this unique material is found in the birth and resurrection narratives.

Here is where our study of *All the Music of the Bible* comes back into sharp focus: Luke's distinctive telling of the stories of Elizabeth, Mary, Zechariah, John and Jesus are half-told, half-sung! Nowhere else in the New Testament is found such a single concentration of song, liturgy, praise, and exultation as that found in the first two chapters of Luke's gospel.

Mary responds to Elizabeth's prophecy with the words, "My soul magnifies the Lord" (1:46 NRSV) After falling mute following the news that Elizabeth was to conceive, Zechariah's tongue was loosed, and he pronounced the blessing, "Blessed is the LORD God of Israel for He has visited and redeemed His people" (1:68 NKJV) words now called the *Benedictus,* or "blessing."

When Mary delivered, a host of angels sang before a band of shepherds, "Glory to God in the highest, and on earth peace, good will toward men" (2:14 NKJV)

And again, Simeon broke into joyful praise with the words, "Lord, now You are letting Your servant depart in peace, according to Your word" (v. 29 NKJV) when the young Jesus was presented at the temple. A faithful servant of the Lord, Simeon knew he had seen the Savior whose coming had been foretold. Only once in the Epistles does the New Testament record early Christian songs and hymns apart from those that comprise the birth narratives and songs we find in The Revelation of John. For this reason, we turn now to the Gospel of Luke.

The "Magnificat"

Luke 1:46–55

When Mary greeted Elizabeth, the baby in Elizabeth's womb leaped. Elizabeth knew this was a sign; she blessed Mary and her unborn child, and spoke confidently a prophecy about the coming Messiah. Mary responded in poetry, one of the most beloved of passages of New Testament Scripture. Mary's song of praise found in Luke 1:46–55, traditionally called the *Magnificat* from the Latin meaning *to magnify,* has been set to music by composers throughout the centuries with perhaps none more masterful than that by J. S. Bach. From the opening lines, *My soul magnifies the Lord, and my spirit rejoices in God my Savior,* throughout the carefully scripted ten verses comprising this text, we find a distinctive characteristic of ancient Hebrew poetry, consistent with enduring Scriptures in Isaiah, Psalms and other Old Testament poetic passages.

The *Magnificat* is written in the perfect tense, a grammatical construction in the original Greek signifying a past completed action that has ongoing or enduring consequences. As Mary proclaims these words, she is but a young girl, betrothed to be married to an honorable man, who finds herself expecting a child—with nothing more to go on than an angel's visitation. Yet Mary yielded herself completely to God's will and sings with an unwavering confidence that what had been proclaimed and promised had *already* come to pass. Mary praised God as if what He had declared had been fully accomplished—months before the child was even born! What a marvelous poem of rejoicing the *Magnificat* is!

Just as Hannah spoke thus when God came to her in the grief born of a barren womb, so Mary sings of the reversal of human fortunes; she praises the Mighty One who lifts up the lowly and brings down the powerful; she declares once again her faith in the Sovereign God who intervenes in human history to bring salvation to His people.

Mary's hymn speaks of her own humility; she was mindful of her status as a humble village maiden whose "low estate" (v. 48 KJV) the

Lord regarded. Mary's firstborn child was to say of himself: "I am meek and lowly in heart" (Matt. 11:29 KJV). Such poverty of spirit is the first beatitude and the very threshold of the kingdom of heaven. By speaking of her "low estate," Mary beautifully anticipates the low estate of our Lord's royal birth, something that can come only from the intervening hand of God. As with Mary, let us pray these words in perfect tense, declaring once again the salvation God promised has indeed come to pass!

And Mary said,

My soul magnifies the Lord, and my spirit rejoices in God my Savior,

For for he has looked with favor on the lowliness of his servant. Surely, from now on all generations will call me blessed;

for the Mighty One has done great things for me, and holy is his name.

His mercy is for those who fear him from generation to generation.

He has shown strength with his arm; he has scattered the proud in the thoughts of their hearts.

He has brought down the powerful from their thrones, and lifted up the lowly;

he has filled the hungry with good things, and sent the rich away empty.

He has helped his servant Israel, in remembrance of his mercy,

according to the promise he made to our ancestors, to Abraham and to his descendants forever. (Luke 1:46–55 NRSV)

Benedictus

Luke 1:68–79

The loosening of Zechariah's tongue at the naming ceremony was nothing less than miraculous, yet another astounding event in a lengthy list of unexpected, awe-inspiring events surrounding the birth of the Christ child. Elizabeth's child was born, ending her shame as a barren woman, for in that day and time, barrenness was viewed as a sign of falling out of God's favor. Following God's instruction, yet acting against the customs of the day, *this* child would not be named after his father, Zechariah, but would be called John. Despite the objections of neighbors and relatives, whose participation in the naming and blessing of a child was customary, Zechariah insisted on the name John as Elizabeth had spoken when Zechariah was without words.

As we are told in verse 64, immediately Zechariah's "mouth was opened and his tongue freed" (NRSV). This pious priest who had been unable to speak for the duration of Elizabeth's pregnancy suddenly began to prophesy. He "was filled with the Holy Spirit" (NRSV) and spoke the words of prophecy traditionally called the *Benedictus,* after the first word of the Latin translation meaning "blessed."

This song of thanksgiving naturally falls into two parts. The first (vv. 68–75) is a song of thanksgiving for the Messianic hopes of the Jewish nation. The second part (vv. 76–79) is an address by Zechariah to his son, declaring publicly that this child was to play an important role in the redemption of the world, proclaiming repentance for the forgiveness of sins and the salvation yet to come. Of course, as we know so well, this child born of prophecy and proclamation, who "grew and became strong in spirit" (v. 80 NRSV) was indeed John the Baptist and preached about the remission of sins. Today, Zechariah's *Benedictus* is spoken at funeral services around the world at the moment of interment, when words of thanksgiving for redemption are offered as an expression of Christian hope.

> Blessed be the Lord God of Israel, for he has looked favorably
> on his people and redeemed them.
>
> He has raised up a mighty savior for us in the house of his
> servant David,
> As he spoke through the mouth of his holy prophets from of
> old,
> that we would be saved from our enemies and from the hand of
> all who hate us.

Thus he has shown the mercy promised to our ancestors, and
    has remembered his holy covenant,
the oath that he swore to our ancestor Abraham, to grant us
that we, being rescued from the hands of our enemies, might
    serve him without fear,
in holiness and righteousness before him all our days.

And you, child, will be called the prophet of the Most High;
    for you will go before the Lord to prepare his ways,
to give knowledge of salvation to his people by the forgiveness of
    their sins.

By the tender mercy of our God, the dawn from on high will
    break upon us,
to give light to those who sit in darkness and in the shadow of
    death,
to guide our feet into the way of peace.
(Luke 1:68–79 NRSV)

Gloria in Excelsis

Luke 2:10–14

"Music is well said to be the speech of angels," noted Thomas
Carlyle, a seventeenth century English historian. That statement could
never be truer than with the *Gloria in Excelsis*. This text, also called the
Song of Angels, was sung by a host of angels when the Christ child was
born. To discover the treasure in these simple lines, we must first take
leave of the Gospel of Luke and look briefly at the Gospel of Matthew.

Luke tells the story of Jesus' birth from Mary's point of view; Matthew recounts the events from Joseph's perspective. Matthew then
moves immediately to the visit of the three Wise Men, giving greatest
importance to making the birth of the Messiah known to kings and
rulers, the rich and powerful, thus fulfilling the prophesy of Isa. 7:14.
However, Luke's account of Jesus' birth fulfills the words of Isa. 61:1–3,
proclaiming the news of the Savior's birth first to the poor and power-
less. Let us not fail to recognize that the Song of Angels fills the air from
a multitude of heavenly hosts only *after* the angel declares the sign will
be nothing majestic, regal, or triumphant. No, the sign will be a small

baby lying in a feed trough. Luke alone tells us the angelic Messenger calls this child "Savior," a title found in no other Gospel. Without hesitation then, and with the full assurance of angels and prophets, we can join with the heavenly hosts in praising God, and singing,

> Glory to God in the highest heaven, and on earth peace among
> those whom he favors! (Luke 2:14 NRSV)

The "Nunc Dimittis"

Luke 2:29–32

On the eighth day following his birth, Jesus' parents took him to Jerusalem. As they entered the temple, they met Simeon, a "righteous and devout" man who had waited his entire life to see this child, whom Simeon believed to be the "consolation of Israel" (Luke 2:25 NIV). Taking Jesus in his arms, Simeon declared Jesus to be the salvation of the world when he sang this inspired prayer known as the *Nunc Dimittis* from the Latin for *now you are dismissing*. These words of adoration and prophecy are lines also found in Isa. 52:10, Ps. 98:2, and Isa. 49:6.

> Master, now you are dismissing your servant in peace, according
> to your word;
> for my eyes have seen your salvation,
> which you have prepared in the presence of all peoples,
> a light for revelation to the Gentiles and for glory to your people
> Israel.
> (Luke 2:29–32 NRSV)

The fervent praise of an old man is rich in spiritual suggestion. This spectator of the most significant baby of all history kept the lamp of prophecy burning when religion was at a low ebb in Israel. Simeon means "one who hears and obeys," and indeed, he was. Simeon knew the voice speaking through the prophets of old. He obeyed the leading of the Holy Spirit when he came to the temple on the day of Jesus' presentation. Coming into the temple, he took the babe in his arms and blessed God. What a wonderful benediction were these words!

At last his faith had been fulfilled and Simeon could die in peace. He had seen the salvation of the Lord. Simeon was not ashamed to declare that the One born in the city of David was the Savior of the world, something the learned scribes and religious leaders of his time failed to discern. Rather than welcoming the coming of the Messiah with wonder and praise, the scribes looked upon Jesus as one who stirred up trouble, one who challenged the accepted order of the day. For them, Jesus would become a stumbling stone, a rock of offense. Simeon warned Mary and Joseph "this child is destined for the falling and the rising of many in Israel . . . a sign that will be opposed. . . ." (v. 34 NRSV) Simeon's faithfulness, however, was greatly rewarded. He knew that Mary's child was the One who would bless the world, and to this day, his words are often spoken as the benediction at the close of Christian worship in services around the world.

Paul's Exhortation to Sing

Though, sadly, we are given few details on the music of the early church, there is no doubt that the apostles and first-century Christians were well acquainted with hymns, and the use of song in worship was a common practice whenever Christians gathered together. Some scholars believe that the Apostle Paul may have written many of the early hymns. In fact, numerous passages from Paul's epistles seem to be quotations from hymns or psalms that were likely well known to the early believers. Passages such as Eph. 5:14 follow a perfect hymn pattern in construct and rhythm when read in the original language:

> Awake, O sleeper,
> rise up from the dead,
> and Christ will give you light.
> (Eph. 5:14 NLT)

As Paul himself wrote to the Christians in Corinth, Ephesus, and Colossae, singing was as natural and necessary to spiritual life as prayer and praise:

- I will pray with the spirit, and I will also pray with the understanding. I will sing with the Spirit, and I will also sing with the understanding. (1 Cor. 14:15 NKJV)

- And do not be drunk with wine, in which is dissipation; but be filled with the Spirit; speaking to one another in psalms and hymns and spiritual songs, singing and making melody in your heart to the Lord. (Eph. 5:18–19 NKJV)

- Let the word of Christ dwell in you richly in all wisdom, teaching and admonishing one another in psalms and hymns and spiritual songs, singing with grace in your hearts to the Lord. (Col. 3:16 NKJV)

Of course, James added his word of approval when he said, "Is anyone cheerful? Let him sing psalms" (5:13 NKJV).

Contemporary writer and theologian Robert Webber, a noted scholar of Christian worship, writes:

> Though the New Testament does not give any detailed information on the structure of the first Christian services, it leaves little room for doubt concerning the basic elements of primitive worship: prayer, praise, confession of sin, confession of faith, Scripture reading and preaching, the Lord's Supper, and the collection. Early descriptions of Christian worship, such as that in Justin's *Apology*, reveal a close similarity to the practice of the synagogue. Even without the synagogue model, however, the fundamental elements would surely have found a place, and distinctive Christian features would have their own origin.[1]

However, we are told in several instances that Paul himself sang to the Lord. For example, as he and Silas sang hymns to God while imprisoned in the deepest innermost dungeon, their feet clamped in stocks and their backs bleeding from merciless flogging, suddenly Macedonia was shaken with a great earthquake and God blew open their prison door (Acts 16:23–34). Surely we can attest to the power of singing by those who believe!

Into this dearth of details regarding music and song from the early Christians, however, is one notable exception, the pre-Pauline Christ hymn recorded in the epistle written to the Philippians, a letter in which joy and rejoicing are given repeated emphasis. Though scholars contest to this day the authorship and background of this hymn, several things we do know with certainty. We know this hymn was used frequently in early Christian worship. We know these six verses are among the earliest writings that witness to the life, purpose, and mission of Jesus Christ. Here in these words of humility and obedience, exultation and praise, are the lines of one of the earliest Christological hymns. The first of these two clearly distinct stanzas speaks of Christ's life and death; the second speaks of his resurrection. The author of these lyrics took the elemental facts of the gospel and gave us a hymn with concluding lines heard literally around the world:

> Who, being in very nature God,
> did not consider equality with God something to be grasped,
>
> but made himself nothing,
> taking the very nature of a servant,
> being made in human likeness.
>
> And being found in appearance as a man,
> he humbled himself
> and became obedient to death—
> even death on a cross!
>
> Therefore God exalted him to the highest place
> and gave him the name that is above every name,
>
> that at the name of Jesus every knee should bow, in heaven and
> on earth and under the earth,
>
> and every tongue confess that Jesus Christ is Lord,
> to the glory of God the Father. (Phil. 2:6–11 NIV)

Amen! And again we sing, Amen!

Songs of John's Revelation

Studying *All the Music of the Bible* has taken us from reviewing sacred history to hearing prophetic voices, from praying ancient prayers to reviewing the stories of God's mighty acts. One cannot study the musical legacy from Genesis to Revelation without marvelling anew at

God's amazing grace. To undertake a study of the richness of music in the Holy Scriptures is to study nothing less than the history of salvation itself. Yet our work is not yet complete. Until we conclude with the evocative, dramatic visions of John of Patmos, we have not finished the task we began with our study of Abraham and music in ancient Hebrew practices.

No other book in the Old or New Testaments has been the subject of as much misuse and misinterpretation as the book of Revelation, nor has any other book of the Bible inspired such anxiety and fear. From the 1970 publication of *The Late Great Planet Earth* to the ill-fated predictions of the coming end times by countless fundamentalists, The Revelation to John has often been used to evoke fear of the end times among modern-day believers and non-believers alike. It is with nothing less than absolute confidence that I can assure you, this was not the author's purpose or intent.

Clearly using a first-person narrative, the writer of Revelation was quite familiar with the struggle and hardship of the seven Anatolian churches near the end of the first century. Calling himself their "brother" (1:9), John identifies himself as one who shares in their persecution. He clearly states that he "was in the spirit on the Lord's day" (1:10 NRSV) when he heard a voice telling him to "write in a book what you see and send it to the seven churches, to Ephesus, to Smyrna, to Pergamum, to Thyatira, to Sardis, to Philadelphia, and to Laodicea" (v. 11).

In a time of rampant persecution, this book was written to bring hope, encouragement and comfort to Christians living under terribly difficult circumstances. In fact, no sooner than John identifies himself as God's servant does John pen a blessing on "the one who reads" (v. 3) this book. Do we even need to state the obvious? Oh yes, we do. Because of the frequent misuse of this book in the hands of well-intentioned Christians, we do indeed need to state the obvious: a blessing is never intended to produce fear and anxiety, especially for followers of Christ! Before the first chapter ends, the message is clear: "Do not be afraid; I am the first and the last" (v. 17).

Without a doubt, the language, symbolism, and imagery found in these twenty-two chapters are unfamiliar, confusing, and perhaps alarming to some. However, one need read no further than the introduction included in almost any study Bible to realize that this final book of the Bible is quite distinctive in language, purpose, and intent. Revelation stands alone in the New Testament as the only book written in the ancient style of writing called "apocalypse." This categorization is taken directly from the first two opening words, "The revelation of Jesus Christ." The Greek word for "revelation," *apokalypsis,* is no doubt used by John to indicate the nature of what's to come for "the one who reads aloud the words of the prophecy . . . who hear and who keep what is written in it" (v. 3).

An apocalypse is a revelation of God's truth given to a human through a mediating heavenly or angelic messenger. Only in the Old Testament book of Daniel do we find another book-length apocalyptic work in the Bible, which interestingly is also written to God's chosen people during a time of great persecution.

The language, symbolism, and imagery that make Revelation so unusual are actually quite purposeful. Because John was writing to Christians suffering great oppression, he wrote in language that would be unfamiliar and obtuse to those outside the faith, drawing heavily from Old Testament imagery, symbol, and worship so the faithful could understand the message of hope. For the seven Anatolian churches (a region in modern-day Turkey), The Revelation to John was what we might call a "code" book, written to say that the Kingdom of God is fully present, both now and forever—a message as meaningful for churches today as it was then!

From the deep bass tones and tight harmonies of Southern Gospel quartets singing "John, the Revelator" to the indescribable beauty of Handel's *Messiah,* images from The Revelation to John fill our worship today. We can almost hear George Frideric Handel's quill scratching down the notes to "Worthy is the Lamb" from his *Messiah* as we read from these passages in Rev. 5.

Sixteen hymn or hymn-like compositions are found in the section starting with 4:1 through 22:7, the longest section of Revelation. Beginning in 4:1, the focus of John's vision moves from earth to heaven as he sees an open door and is ushered into the heavenly throne room, and from there John unfolds his prophetic vision. The words that come to us across the centuries from the small island of Patmos are a *single* prophetic vision, not a series of multiple visions, although they are recorded in seven overlapping or "interlocking" vision cycles. Therefore, this is the book of "Revelation," *singular,* not *Revelations,* plural, as is often misquoted. The entirety of this work is but a single vision with a single purpose: to strengthen and encourage those who were oppressed and persecuted. Included in the hymns in this section are two single hymns (15:3–4 and 12:10–12) and seven antiphonal songs (4:8–11; 5:9–14; 7:9–12; 11:15–18; 16:5–7; and 19:1–4, 5–8).

> Holy, holy, holy,
> the Lord God the Almighty,
> who was and is and is to come.
>
> And whenever the living creatures give glory and honor and thanks to the one who is seated on the throne, who lives forever and ever, the twenty-four elders fall before the one who is seated on the throne and worship the one who lives forever and ever; they cast their crowns before the throne, singing,
>
> You are worthy, our Lord and God
> to receive glory and honor and power,
> for you created all things, and by your will they existed and were
>   created.
> (Rev. 4:8–11 NRSV)

Holy, holy, holy. What these three words have inspired! One of the most beloved hymns quickly comes to mind with the utterance of these three words:

> Holy, holy, holy!
> All the saints adore thee,
>
> Casting down their golden crowns
> around the glassy sea;
>
> Cherubim and seraphim
> falling down before thee,
>
> Which wert and art and evermore shalt be.[2]

In these lines of worshipful hymnody we find language and symbol from John's vision, words which bring to mind similar words from the prophet Isaiah:

> I saw the Lord sitting on a throne, high and lofty . . .
> Holy, holy, holy is the LORD of hosts;
> The whole earth is full of his glory.
> (Isa. 6:1, 3 NRSV)

The use of hymns in Revelation often serves to summarize or reinforce the central message of the vision. In this hymn, that message is clearly God's holiness, that God alone is worthy of praise.

From Hebrew antiquity to our own present day worship, the language of holiness and praise transcends time for all those who call upon the Lord. Biblically, the word *holy* means "set apart," from the Latin, *sanctus,* from which we get the word *sanctify.* The use of the thrice holy title, as used throughout the Old Testament and found again in Revelation, has come to be called the Sanctus in the church. It is that part of the service often spoken immediately before the communion.

The New Song

Let's put ourselves in the scene described in Rev. 4. Imagine a heavenly throne room, described to us laden with Old Testament imagery as vivid as any we've discussed. A member of the Translations Committee of the American Bible Society, Richard L. Jeske, notes a few of the Old Testament images included in John's description:

> Jasper and carnelian are among the stones of paradise [Ezekiel 28:13]. . . . The rainbow around God's throne recalls the promise to Noah. . . . The 24 elders on 24 thrones (4:4) reflect the ancient idea of the heavenly court. . . . The number 24 also suggests the totality of God's people, a combination of 12 patriarchs and 12 apostles. . . .[3]

Every line of John's description is alive, pulsating with vibrant images and awe-inspiring creatures. Read this passage. How brilliant is the throne from where you're standing? Once John has established the glory and wonder of the heavenly throne room and the holiness of God, he offers his readers this antiphonal hymn. Asking the question,

"Who is worthy?" (5:2), this song offers the answer we know to be true: only God is worthy. The hymn in these verses introduces the concept or image of the "Lamb who was slain." Occurring 28 times, "the Lamb who was slain" is the single most dominant image in the book of Revelation. This hymn establishes one of the primary messages of Revelation—that only the crucified Christ, "the Lamb who was slain" (NIV) is worthy.

> You are worthy to take the scroll and to open its seals, for you were slaughtered and by your blood you ransomed for God saints from every tribe and language and people and nation;
>
> you have made them to be a kingdom and priests serving our God, and they will reign on earth.
>
> Then I looked, and I heard the voice of many angels surrounding the throne and the living creatures and the elders; they numbered myriads of myriads and thousands of thousands,
>
> singing with full voice, "Worthy is the Lamb that was slaughtered to receive power and wealth and wisdom and might and honor and glory and blessing!"
>
> Then I heard every creature in heaven and on earth and under the earth and in the sea, and all that is in them, singing,
>
> "To the one seated on the throne and to the Lamb be blessing and honor and glory and might forever and ever!"
>
> And the four living creatures said, "Amen!" And the elders fell down and worshiped.
> (Rev. 5:9–14 NRSV)

This is the new song, the new covenant. The Old Testament speaks often of a "new song," a song of salvation, such as when the psalmist wrote, "O sing to the LORD a new song; sing to the LORD, all the earth. Sing to the LORD, bless his name; tell of his salvation from day to day" (Ps. 96:1–2 NRSV). Here, however, the singers are united as the "living beings" and the "elders," the people of God of all generations. All who have been redeemed by the blood of the Lamb, who was killed but now lives forever and ever, cry out together: "Worthy is the Lamb!"

This doxology, thus begun by the church, and carried on by the angels, is resounded and echoed by the whole creation, v. 13. Heaven and earth ring with the high praises of the Redeemer. The whole creation fares the better for Christ . . . that part . . . is made for the whole creation is a song of *blessing, and honor, and glory, and power.* . . . We worship and glorify one and the same God for our creation and for our redemption. . . . Thus we have seen this sealed [scroll] passing with great solemnity from the hand of the Creator into the hand of the Redeemer.[4]

The Song of the Lamb

The sea of glass mingled with fire sets the scene for this song. A hymn of praise, this song continues the theme of worthiness, that only the Lamb who was slain is worthy, but here in these words, God the Creator and Christ the Redeemer are worshipped together. A great multitude with harps sings the glorious triumphs of the Lamb. The Lord Jesus had gained redemption for all people by His death on the cross and resurrection. Here those who have gained the victory sing the "Song of Moses," words of praise dating back to when the Israelites passed victoriously through the Red Sea and saw all their enemies destroyed by the miraculous power of God,

The Song of the Lamb is the very Song of Moses, adapted to those who are delivered from sin by the Lamb of God who takes away the sins of the world.

> Great and marvelous are Your works, Lord God Almighty!
> Just and true are Your ways, O King of the saints!

> Who shall not fear You, O Lord, and glorify Your name?
> For You alone are holy.
> For all nations shall come and worship before You,
> For your judgments have been manifested. (Rev. 15:3–4 NKJV)

The Hymn of Victory

After these things I heard a loud voice of a great multitude in heaven, saying,

Alleluia!
Salvation and glory and honor and power belong to the Lord
our God! (Rev. 19:1 NKJV)

The vision is nearing its conclusion, and heaven exults! These lines from Revelation open the final words of song in the New Testament. The message is clear: God's judgments are true and righteous. The twenty-four elders, John's symbol for all of God's people, and the four creatures, used throughout Revelation as the symbol for all of creation, now sing "Amen! Alleluia!"

Through much of chapter 18, John writes poetically, a dirge of harsh words lamenting the fall of Babylon. Using a metaphor for Rome, this lament of Babylon is prophetic, anticipating the fall of Rome. Those who have turned away from God, choosing instead "a dwelling place" for every "foul . . . bird" and "hateful beast" (NRSV) living in decadent luxury, sin, and drunkenness will suffer "death and mourning and famine" (v. 8 NKJV).

It is, however, worthy of restating the most important point to remember when studying Revelation: Old Testament imagery is prevalent in every line, every stanza, and every paragraph. Phrases, motifs, symbols, and language from Isaiah, Ezekiel, Jeremiah, Zechariah, and of course, the first five books of the Bible (the Pentateuch) are all images that were quite well known and familiar to the Christians in the seven churches to which John is writing. John makes use of traditional Jewish and Christian elements such as Alleluia (or Hallelujah, from the Hebrew phrase or "formula" meaning "praise Yahweh"), "Amen," for "so be it" or "let it be so," the Sanctus (Holy, holy, holy), doxologies (from the same root as dogma), to name but a few.

As John moves through the song of lament in chapter 18, the final hymn in chapter 19 brings the reader back to the message for Christians. The words of this last song affirm that God is in his heavens, that we are God's saints and servants, and "these are true words of God" (19:9 NRSV)

And from the throne came a voice saying,

"Praise our God, all you his servants,
and all who fear him, small and great."

Then I heard what seemed to be the voice of a great multitude,
like the sound of many waters and like the sound of mighty
thunderpeals, crying out,

"Hallelujah!
For the Lord our God the Almighty reigns.

Let us rejoice and exult and give him the glory,
for the marriage of the Lamb has come,
and his bride has made herself ready;

to her it has been granted to be clothed
with fine linen, bright and pure." (19:5–8 NRSV)

And finally, just as John began, he completes his vision with specific blessings for those who believe (20:6, 22:7, 22:14). From this song
of victory in 19:1–8, John's prophetic voice is one of praise, proclaiming that God's "words are trustworthy and true" (21:5 NRSV), the victory is sure, the Kingdom of God is, indeed, at hand!

The Spirit and the bride say,
"Come."

And let everyone who hears say,
"Come."

And let everyone who is thirsty
come.

Let anyone who wishes take the water of life as a gift.
(Rev. 22:17 NRSV)

Let us conclude with the confident benediction of The Revelator:
"The grace of the Lord Jesus be with all the saints. Amen." (Rev. 22:21
NRSV) And Amen!

12

The Birth of the Modern Hymn

Music, of all the arts the one nearest the human religious impulse, was admitted early to Christian activity because it provided a language for the deepest expressions of the soul. —H. T. McElrath

MUSIC MAKES THE WORD memorable and has been used for that purpose throughout Christian history. Early Christians were singing Christians, of that there is no doubt. But the nature of *what* Christians were to sing became one of the most significant controversies of the early Church and continued to cause discord for centuries. And what was the issue at the center of this controversy? Whether or not songs worthy of Christian worship could be composed by individuals—or must the songs, choruses and hymns sung in worship come directly from quoted Scripture?

The printed hymnal as we know it is relatively new to worship when one looks at the totality of Christian history. In fact, we might not even have those hymnals available to us each Sunday, if the controversy surrounding music in the early church had been resolved differently!

After the events surrounding the death and resurrection of Jesus, the followers of Christ (not yet called Christians) began meeting in small groups, apart from the Jewish synagues, yet still observing many of the Jewish worship practices. Readings from Scripture, singing, and recitations of proverbs and verses were common to the early church gatherings. But the early church soon began to take on the image and likeness of Christ, and distinctions between Jewish and Christian worship came within the first century.

The Synod of Laodicea in A.D. 363 stated that psalms composed by individuals must not be used in the church, and again in 563, the church council of Braga, Portugal, forbade the singing of any hymn except a psalm of David. Not until A.D. 633 did an ecclesiastical trial in Toledo, Spain, rule, "Surely there is no more ground condemning man-composed hymns than man-composed prayers." Nevertheless the controversy lasted for more than a thousand years, reaching well into the worship services of the Puritans, and in some denominations, this controversy continues to influence worship still today.

A Brief History of Hymnody

Early historians left accounts of singing by first century Christians. As early as A.D. 112, in a letter to the Roman emperor, Pliny explained the "contagion" of Christianity had penetrated much of the area to which he was assigned, reporting "they have a custom of meeting before dawn on an appointed day, and singing by turn hymns to Christ."[1] In a letter to a friend, church father and historian Tertullian objected to the marriage of a Christian and a non-Christian "because they could not sing together. Whereas, if he would marry a Christian, then between the two would echo psalms and hymns, each challenging the other as to which shall better chant the praises of the Lord."[2]

By definition, a hymn is scriptural, is easily sung, has a definite message to communicate, and is clearly God- or Christ-centered. Though hymns as we know them today combine the essential elements of rhythm, melody and harmony, these elements did not appear in early hymnody for quite possibly one of the most obvious of reasons: few people could read or write—even among royalty in many areas! Although we find evidence that the Greeks had some rudimentary form of musical notation, the advent of staff notation did not occur until the eleventh century. Until then, musicians of the church had no form of musical notation available, and even then, only the educated clergy could make use of it.

In early church history, the most widespread form of worship music was Gregorian chant, also known as *plainsong*, simple chant formulas consisting of monophonic (a pure, unharmonized melody) music with Latin text. Similar forms of chant employed across Europe, Russia and as far reaching as Asia Minor came from many sources, among which was a form called *psalm tones* that date back to some of the earliest known liturgical expressions of the church.

By the ninth century, we find the beginnings of polyphonic music, that is, music with more than one melodious line, which became the rudimentary advent of harmony in worship music and became known as *organum*. Still, worship (the mass) was *observed*, not structured to allow or encourage congregational participation.

Ancient Irish Harp from the Eleventh Century[3]
Figure 12.1 from a plaster cast in the Victoria and Albert Museum

Yet the worshipful hearts of fervent believers could not be contained. The innate response to salvation cannot abide without song. The lower classes were not without music of their own! Joy and sorrow, gratitude and grief, hope and despair—all find their most poignant expression in song. Alongside the fine art music evolving among the learned clergy and high artistry of church musicians came a much simpler form of musical expression: the development of folk art music. With the influence of St. Francis of Assisi in the twelfth century came simpler songs of praise and devotion. These two forms of Christian song—the fine art music of the church, the clergy, and the well-to-do; and the folk art music of the masses—continued to evolve along class lines until the Reformation. As one scholar states:

> In some respects the Protestant Reformation was a surfacing of a great underground movement of popular religious song. Luther and Calvin both sought to magnify the singing of the common folk. . . . This was also the period of the rise and growth of liturgical organ music. . . . The culmination of these developments was the consummate work of Johann Sebastian Bach (1685–1750).[4]

In *The New International Dictionary of the Christian Church,* J. B. MacMillan also lauds Bach's unparalleled artistry, saying that the great repertory of organ music based on choral melodies reached "its height of attainment with the creative genius of J. S. Bach in the eighteenth century. Indeed, J. S. Bach was the last truly great genius to whom music for the sancturary was his major concern."[5]

The Protestant Reformation brought about the confluence of social, historical, political and religious events that gave birth to congregational singing and the free, unhindered development of Christian music. We can see the results of the loosening of restraint both in the classical (fine art) renderings of sophisticated works such as Handel's *Messiah* (1741) or Mozart's *Requiem* (1791), and in the simpler folk art music from which evolved the revival hymns of Charles Wesley and later the gospel music popularized by the evangelical tours of Dwight L. Moody. (For an extensive list of Christian hymns, see Appendix E.) Too numerous to mention are the early saints and reformers, monks and mystics, skilled musicians and humble servants, whose songs and prayers of devotion formed the legacy from which come our treasured hymns. We must, nonetheless, mention but a few.

Hymnists of the Early Church

Clement of Alexandria

One of the earliest hymn writers of whom there is any record and our first known Christian scholar was Clement of Alexandria (A.D. 150–220). Born in Athens in A.D. 150 of aristocratic parentage, he traveled to Alexandria to study in the city's famous libraries. While there he came under the influence of a Christian and was gloriously converted. A powerful preacher of the gospel, he also composed many hymns before he died a martyr's death in A.D. 220.

In a letter to a friend, Clement once wrote: "We cultivate our fields, praising; we sail the sea, hymning. Our lives are filled with prayers and praises and Scripture readings, before meals and before bed, and even during the night. By this means we unite ourselves to the Heavenly choir!"

One of his compositions, "Shepherd of Tender Youth" is, in fact, still in use in Europe.

Ambrose of Milan

The son of a Praetorian guardsman, Ambrose (A.D. 339–397) studied law and later was appointed the Roman governor of Milan. Eventually he became the bishop of that city and taught theology. Known as the father of Latin hymnography, he wrote the famous Latin hymn "Christ the Splendor of the Father's Glory," as well as "A Hymn of the Dawn" and "On the First Day." Though his contribution to hymnody is evident even today, he is best known as the one who greatly influenced Augustine, which is worthy of note because Martin Luther's convictions and theology were largely shaped by the writings of Augustine. The roots of Luther's impassioned belief that we are saved by faith and faith alone is readily apparent in these few lines from Ambrose's hymn, "Christ the Splendor."

> Christ is the splendor of the Father's glory.
> He is the true son,
> come down with sparkling gleams and radiance.
> We must set aside our sinful guilt

and by grace and faith
grow in our faith until it is strong again.
Christ will, through grace and the Spirit,
lead us in days of rejoicing.
We will be filled with the Holy Spirit,
and our faith will grow like the midday sun.
For the Son is complete in the Father,
and the Father is complete in the Word.

Romanos of Constantinople

Recognized as a great hymn-writer of the early sixth century, Saint Romanus (also known as "Melodus") wrote over 1,000 hymns, though only approximately eighty survived. He served as a deacon in the Church of the Resurrection in Beirut, and later became pastor of the large church in Constantinople (A.D. 491–518). According to legend, he fell asleep on Christmas Eve and was commanded by an angel to write a Christmas hymn called, "The Nativity," based on 1 Timothy 3:16. The lines from this hymn quoted here bear a striking similarity to phrases from the Apostle's Creed, a confession of faith dating back to the *Apostolic Tradition* of Hippolytus (c. 215) in its earliest form, and again in a Greek version by Marcellus of Ancyra (c. 340).

> Christ was revealed in the flesh
> Vindicated by the Holy Spirit
> Seen by angels
> Believed on by the world
> And ascended into heaven
> How deep and how rich is our historical heritage as Christians!

John of Damascus

John (A.D. 675–749) began his preaching in Damascus and later entered the monastery on Mount Tabor (the Mount of Transfiguration). He composed many early hymns. "The Life Giving Cross," a short hymn of thirteen lines, holds the cross before our eyes as the giver of life and presents the resurrection as the way back to heaven. "The Presentation of the Lord" is based on the presentation of Jesus in the temple (Luke 2:21–38). John writes, "Today, the gate of heaven opens, for the Father's word, without beginning. A child of nearly forty days is carried into the temple. An old man receives him and exclaims, 'My eyes have seen your salvation—salvation for all mankind.'"

Bernard of Clairvaux

Saint Bernard (A.D. 1090–1152) founded the monastery of Clairvaux, where he exhorted applicants, "If you desire to enter here, leave at the threshold the body you have brought with you from the world; here there is room only for your soul." Called "the best monk who ever lived" by Martin Luther, Bernard organized the second Crusade to the Holy Land and wrote many well-known hymns. Renowned as the sweetest hymn of the Middle Ages was his hymn, "Jesus Thou Joy of Loving Hearts," though it is Bernard's song to Christ's body on the cross (translated in 1656 by John Gearhart) that has truly stood the test of time:

O sacred Head, now wounded,
With grief and shame weighed down,
Now scornfully surrounded
With thorns, Thine only crown;
O Sacred Head, what glory,
What bliss till now was thine!
Yet, though despised and gory,
I joy to call Thee mine.

O noblest Brow and dearest,
In other days the world,
All feared when thou appearest;
What shame on Thee is hurled!
How art thou pale with anguish,
with sore abuse and scorn!
How doth Thy visage languish
that once was bright as morn!

What Thou, my Lord, hast suffered,
Was all for sinners' gain;
Mine, mine was the transgression,

But Thine the deadly pain.
Lo, here I fall, my Savior!
'Tis I deserve Thy place;
Look on me with Thy favor,
Vouchsafe to me Thy grace.

What language shall I borrow
To thank Thee, dearest friend,
For this Thy dying sorrow,
Thy pity without end?
O make me Thine forever,
And should I fainting be,
Lord, let me never, never
Outlive my love to Thee.

When strength one day shall fail me,
Lord, fail me not I pray:
When pangs of death assail me,
Beside me, Jesus stay:
When, head and heart I languish,
And hardly draw my breath,
Deliver me from anguish,
By virtue of Thy death.

Be near when I am dying,
O show thy cross to me;
And for my succor flying,
Come, Lord, to set me free.
These eyes new faith receiving,
From Jesus shall not move;
For he who dies believing,
Dies safely through Thy love.

Francis of Assisi

Canonized less than two years after his death, Saint Francis (A.D. 1182–1225) showed unwavering devotion to apostolic poverty that was a powerful example at a time when the church was under fire for its abuses of wealth. When the effects of imprisonment and serious illness at the age of twenty-five brought him to Christ, he became a monk and founded the Franciscan order. His wealthy father disinherited him, and St. Francis lived a life of privation and hardship, but his joyful spirit, love of nature, and songs of praise could not be suppressed. He remains one of the most revered saints to this day.

Saint Francis' most famous hymn, "Canticle to the Sun," is a pious outburst of passionate love for nature, soaring high above other pastorals of the Middle Ages. Indeed, Francis's love for nature is rare in the records of his age and puts him into companionship with that large modern company who see poems in the clouds and hear symphonies in flowers. He loved all the trees, stones, birds, and plants of the field; the rushing waters of rivers and seas, but above all things, he loved the sun and the moon. Believing these two illuminated our eyes by day and provided the source that lights the night, Francis wrote, "God has illuminated our eyes by these two."

The Legacy of the Reformers

As we've already noted, the Protestant Reformation was nothing less than the true wellspring of congregational singing, due in large measure to the lives of three men: the first, a gifted pastor who loved to sing; the second, an impassioned student and teacher of the Bible; and the third, a scholar and churchman. These three shared the conviction that singing belonged to the people, to the believers, and that by participating in worship through "the singing of songs, hymns, and spiritual praises" (Col. 3:16), people grew into a deeper faith. Isn't it interesting that the three reformers most often credited with shaping and influencing the Reformation all shared the deep conviction that music and singing shaped the soul and transformed hearts!

Jan Hus

"We not only preach the gospel from the pulpit, but also by our hymns," stated Jan Hus (1369–1415), the Bohemian reformer whose preaching, writing, and work predated the work of Luther, and indeed, greatly influenced Luther's reforms.

Often known as John Huss, (anglicized spelling), this gifted young man was born in Husinec, a small town in southern Bohemia (now the Czech Republic). Born into poverty, his quick mind did not go unnoticed. Because his mother strongly desired that her son become a priest, Jan was educated and went on to earn his M.A. degree in 1396 from University of Prague—supporting himself by singing! He taught at the university both before and after his ordination as a priest, continuing to serve on the faculty well after he became the rector and preacher at Bethlehem Chapel. Through his powerful sermons, delivered in Czech instead of the traditional Latin, he gained a popular following and became an early advocate of church reform. Condemning church abuses and challenging the church hierarchy, his sermons drew the ire of church officials, and Hus was forbidden to exercise his priestly functions and excommunicated in 1410. He was later condemned at the Council of Constance and burned at the stake.

Although his voice was silenced, his message continued, and the reforms he advocated found their fulfillment in the works and writings of Martin Luther.

Martin Luther

Sola fide, sola gratia, solo scriptura! These words of Martin Luther (1483–1546) are the quintessential summation of this extraordinary man, and in many ways, of the Reformation itself. *Sola fide*—by faith alone are we saved. *Sola gratia*—by grace alone do we live. *Sola scripture*—in the Scripture alone is our faith founded. These were the pillars of all Martin Luther's life, work and theology. These were the three convictions that shaped the man who was largely responsible for the Protestant Reformation.

Born in Eisleben, Germany on November 10, 1483, Luther was the son of a prosperous miner whose personal ambitions included the desire that his son become a lawyer. Honoring his father's wishes, Luther's early education was prepatory for a career in jurisprudence. His decision to enter the Augustinian Monastery in 1505 did not please his earthly father, but no doubt pleased his Heavenly Father. Luther attended the University of Leipzig and later transferred to the University of Wittenberg, where he earned his doctor of theology degree in 1512. Ordained to the priesthood in 1507, this gifted student of the Bible was named Professor of Sacred Scripture at Wittenberg, a post he held until his death.

With more books written about Luther than any other figure in history except Jesus, we can do little justice to the significance of this man's passion for the primacy of Scripture and justification by grace alone. His love of Scripture came from his own intense struggle with questions of faith. He was as pious a priest as any before him, yet still questioned his own personal salvation. Though we don't know the date of his "Tower Experience," the moment at which he came to the clear realization of "salvation by grace alone," we do know Luther's careful reading and study of Scriptures brought him to his knees before the Lord. After the "Tower Experience," Luther wrote, taught, and spoke compellingly, tirelessly, and passionately throughout the rest of his life. He was first and foremost a devout student of the Bible, and it was this life-long study of Scripture that led to his convictions of faith, passion for reform, and power of persuasion.

His love of music is easily overshadowed in deference to the sheer volume of sermons, lectures, correspondence, and theological writings, but this large, robust man who loved life was both a singer and musician of considerable skill. Luther saw music as a gift from God (*Musica Dei donum optimi*), and his leadership in musical reforms centered on the inclusion of all believers in corporate worship. Luther was an avid supporter of the highest art forms of musical expression, as well as musical forms simple enough for a child to sing, as evidenced in his authorship of "Away in a Manger." A man mightily used by God, Luther once said, "What I wish is to make hymns for the people, that the word of God may dwell in their hearts by means of song."

Not one to underestimate the significance of either intellect or emotion in the life of faith, Martin Luther said, "We sing with our heart and mind. We shall be joyful and merry," for Luther firmly believed "music drives away the devil and makes people happy."

Luther played both the lute and the flute (recorder) and wrote many original hymns and chorales, though the exact number is not known for certain. Thirty-eight chorales are attributed to Luther; the best known of these is unquestionably "A Mighty Fortress Is Our God."

With the development of Gutenberg's printing press in 1455, the means for dissemination of Martin Luther's leaflets, treatises, sermons, lectures and songs advanced the cause of church reform. In 1545, Luther published a collection of 101 Christian songs, and his commitment to musical reform in worship did not stop there. Between 1524 and 1545, Luther composed and compiled nine hymnals with the able help of several capable composers and musicians. His work in the compilation of these hymnals was an early prelude to our hymnals today.

Luther's view of music is best summed in his own words from the *Forward* to Georg Rhau's *Symphoniae iucundae,* published in 1538:

> I, Doctor Martin Luther, wish all lovers of the unshackled art of music grace and peace from God the Father and from our Lord Jesus Christ! I truly desire that all Christians would love and regard as worthy the lovely gift of music, which is a precious, worthy, and costly treasure given to mankind by God. The riches of music are so excellent and so precious that words fail me whenever I attempt to discuss and describe them. . . . In summa, next to the Word of God, the noble art of music is the greatest treasure in the world. . . . A person who gives this some thought and yet does not regard music as a marvelous creation of God, must be a clodhopper indeed and does not deserve to be called a human being; he should be permitted to hear nothing but the braying of asses and the grunting of hogs.

John Calvin

John Calvin (1509–1564) knew from an early age that he would become a scholar. The second of five sons of a successful businessman in Paris, he first studied for an ecclesiastical career and later studied law and humanism in the best schools in France. By the time he was twenty-three, he had published his first scholarly work and soon after became involved in the Reformation movement in Paris, an involvement which changed the focus of his academic pursuits. He likely came under the influence of humanist scholars with Protestant leanings and began attending clandestine Protestant meetings. It was there he changed his academic focus and turned his considerable intellect to biblical studies. Though we know very little about Calvin's conversion, of this we can be sure: he soon became one of the leaders of the French Reformation and as such was forced to leave Paris for reasons of personal safety. Traveling widely in France, Switzerland, and Italy to avoid arrest, Calvin nevertheless published the first version of *Institutes of the Christian Religion (Christianae Religionis Insitututio)*, initially a small work by a young reformer of little renown. Calvin intended this work to be nothing more than a short handbook summarizing the new doctrines for the French Protestants; however, God had other plans—both for this small statement of faith and for this reformer on the run. Eventually revised five times, Calvin's *Institutes of the Christian Religion* became the definitive work of the Protestant faith, a work consisting of four volumes with a total of seventy-nine chapters in its final form.

As he matured in the faith and his influence became widespread, Calvin was invited to Geneva to fill a leadership void in the church. Into this city with a widespread reputation for immorality, Calvin poured his considerable energies with the worthy goal of making Geneva a "holy city." It was with this aim that Calvin's life work began in earnest, and his efforts took on much more than religious reform. He played an active role in shaping the governing principles in Geneva. Under his inestimable influence, laws were reformed, making them more humane. A system of universal education for the young was established, and provisions were made for the care of the poor and the elderly. Calvin's influence in politics, aesthetics, science, and history "became so interwoven in Western thought that we must recognize him as one of the great seminal minds . . . in the development of Western culture," writes church historian W. S. Reid in his summation of Calvin's life in *The New International Dictionary of the Christian Church.*

Though both Luther and Calvin worked fervently and ceaselessly for the cause of religious reform, their approach and abilities differed greatly. Where Luther was fiery, zealous, easily stirred to anger, and often lacking in subtlety or tact, Calvin was deliberate, reasoned, and thoughtful. Where Luther consistently engaged in inflammatory polemics readily using coarse humor or crude language to make his point, Calvin sought to organize and consolidate the fractious reform movement. Luther was a biblical theologian who did not try to conform to a system of thought; Luther's passion and thought followed where the Scriptures took him and his own experience of grace became central to all of his thinking. Luther was first and foremost an interpreter of the Word. Calvin, on the other hand, was a systematic theologian for whom the majesty of God was central. Of all that could be said of John Calvin, he was first and foremost a consummate churchman. Biblical scholar, exegetical preacher, pastor and theologian, Calvin was "intense in the service of God, to whom he offered his heart fully."[6] Neither man set out to create a worshipping community apart from the Church of Rome. However, relying on the authority and power of the Holy Scriptures rather than the authority of the pope led both men to decisions of faith that ultimately changed world history. Such is the power of the Word of God!

Though Luther and Calvin shared a deep conviction that worshipful singing should belong to the congregation rather than be restricted to the clergy and skilled musicians, their shared convictions brought them to opposing conclusions. Where Luther believed all music was a gift from God to be used for God's purposes, Calvin urged caution and restraint, recognizing that "there is scarcely in the world anything which is more able to turn or bend this way and that the morals of men" than music. Speaking of the power of music to sway the vagaries of men, Calvin wrote in his lengthy introduction to the *Genevan Psalter:*

> Moreover, because of this, we ought to be the more careful not to abuse it, for fear of soiling and contaminating it, converting it to our condemnation, where it was dedicated to our profit and use. If there were no other consideration than this alone, it ought indeed to move us to moderate the use of music, to make it serve all honest things; and that it should not give occasion for our giving free rein to dissolution, or making ourselves effeminate in disordered delights, and that it should not become the instrument of lasciviousness nor of any shamelessness.

Calvin once wrote to a friend, "Our need is for songs that are not only fun but holy. But none can write them, save he who has received the power of God himself." Calvin worked with the French composer, Marot, and the poet, Beza, to translate the Hebrew Psalms into French, which were published in 1541 with the title *Metrical Psalms*. Well received throughout Europe, sixty-four editions were printed in four years. After Calvin's death, the *Metrical Psalms* became known as the *Genevan Psalter*, a collection that was subsequently translated into many other languages and became the enduring hymnbook for worship in Calvinist towns.

Calvin was very explicit about the power that music had on those who experienced it. Again in the preface to the *Genevan Psalter*, he writes about the power of music.

> Therefore we ought to be even more diligent in regulating it in such a way that it shall be useful to us and in no way pernicious. For this reason the ancient doctors of the Church complain frequently of this, that the people of their times were addicted to dishonest and shameless songs, which not without cause they referred to and called mortal and Satanic poison for corrupting the world. . . . It is true that every bad word (as St. Paul has said) perverts good manner, but when the melody is with it, it pierces the heart much more strongly, and enters into it; in a like manner as through a funnel, the wine is poured into the vessel; so also the venom and the corruption is distilled to the depths of the heart by the melody.

Because of Calvin's deeply felt concern for the salvation of the people, combined with his belief that music could easily become fertile ground for Satan's ploy, he admonished the use of anything for singing in worship but the Holy Scriptures themselves, writing:

> Therefore, when we have looked thoroughly, and searched here and there, we shall not find better songs nor more fitting for the purpose, than the Psalms of David, which the Holy Spirit spoke and made through him. And moreover, when we sing them, we are certain that God puts in our mouths these, as if he himself were singing in us to exalt his glory.

In the areas dominated by Calvin's teachings, "hymns of human composure" were unacceptable, deemed unworthy of the majesty of God, and rejected without exception. However, Luther not only wrote hymns himself, but encouraged and fostered musical training within the church. In the German Reformation, musical artistry and the development of a strong choral repertory flourished. In churches following Calvin's teachings, such was not the case. Strict adherence to the metrical psalms, in effect, restricted any hymnodic creativity or musical mastery in church music, but rather, kept the liturgical emphasis rooted and grounded in Scripture. Both positions on the use of music in the life of the church have enriched our spiritual heritage as Christians.

The Protestant Reformation occurred at a time of sweeping change in the course of human history. As we can clearly see, God used the work of these reformers to transform not only the religious world, but also the world of sacred music. Because of the hard work, sacrifice, diligence, and convictions of these and countless others, we are able to worship freely with greater honesty and spiritual nurture. Though the history of sacred music and hymnody continues well beyond the age of the Reformers, alas, it is here we conclude our study of *All the Music of the Bible,* leaving the works of those who gave us the rich repertory of revival hymns, spirituals, gospel music, anthems, choral texts, cantatas and all the other sacred music we share today to another study of the glorious power of music. However, the next time you sing "A Mighty Fortress is Our God" or "Holy, Holy, Holy," take a moment of thankful prayer, remembering the countless reformers who gave their lives in pursuit of the freedom of worship as we know it today. And all God's people say, "Alleluia! Amen!"

PART 4

■   ■   ■

Pages From My Father's Notes

13

Instrument of Ten Strings

I will sing a new song to you, O God!
I will sing your praises on a ten-stringed harp. —Psalm 144:9 (NLT)

Instrument of Ten Strings[1]

DOUBTLESS DAVID refers to some form of an Assyrian harp in Ps. 144:9, quite probably made of ten strings because the ten fingers would be used to manipulate it. But is there not a deeper significance in the number specified?

The early church fathers felt these ten strings symbolized the Ten Commandments that God gave to Moses, and the four sides of the instrument illustrated the four gospels. Eusebius (A.D. 260–340), commenting on the above verses, says, "The psaltery of ten strings is the worship of the Holy Spirit performed by means of the five senses of the body and by the five powers of the soul." This Eusebius confirms by quoting Paul, "I will sing with my spirit, but I will also sing with my mind (1 Cor. 14:15 NIV). The number, then, can denote the unison of praise ascending to God from all parts of our being.

The underlying thought is that as an instrument is designed for the purpose of praise, so man's chief end is to glorify God. Our whole nature must be absorbed in the supreme task of magnifying the God of all grace. To produce the finest music, more than the strings are necessary. We can think of our human frame as an instrument of ten strings— two hands, two feet, two ears, two eyes, one tongue, one heart—ten in all. Upon this divinely created instrument of ten strings we sing praises unto God, but to praise Him aright it is essential to have:

Two feet to walk in wisdom's narrow way;
Two hands to do His bidding day by day;
Two ears to listen to our loving LORD;
Two eyes to read Jehovah's holy word;
One tongue to tell and sing His worth and grace;
One heart to love Him 'til we see His face.[2]

Two Strings of the Feet

We praise the Lord with the strings of our two feet when we run in the way of His commandments, walk in the spirit, and follow the Lord wherever He may lead. Jesus Himself could praise the Father with the two strings of His feet, for they were crucified feet, even before they were nailed to the cross. After His resurrection, the disciples, beholding the marks of the nails in His feet, worshiped Him as we will do when in heaven we gaze upon those visible scars. Jesus will forever bear the evidence of His anguish in those pierced feet, which never swerved from the pathway of allegiance to the divine will.

Take my feet and let them be
Swift and beautiful for Thee.[3]

One evening before Thomas DeQuince died, he said to his daughter, "I cannot bear the weight of clothes on my feet." Gently she removed the heavy blankets. "Yes, my love," he said, "that is much better. I am better in every way. You know these are the feet Jesus washed."

When he had finished washing their feet, he put on his clothes and returned to his place. (John 13:12 NIV)

Two Strings of the Hands

God is praised with our hands as they engage in holy activity and are employed in diligent and constant service. The word "consecration" means "hands filled." And hands, filled and cleansed, are ever magnifying the Lord.

He who has clean hands will grow stronger and stronger. (Job 17:9 NASB)

Too often life is robbed of harmonious music because we are too close-fisted. The two strings of the hands are shrunken and fail to yield of their substance to Him who opens His hands and satisfies the desire of all who have life.

Crucified hands never make anything shoddy nor touch anything shady. They are never guilty of driving a dishonest bargain or of taking more than a legitimate profit.

Take my hands, and let them move
At the impulse of Thy love.[4]

Two Strings of the Ears

Jesus could praise God with the strings of His ears. In the messianic Ps. 40:6, we read: "My ears you have pierced" (NIV), or "now that you have made me listen." This recalls the liberation of the Israelite slaves in Exodus. Because of the Egyptian slavery, Hebrew law and poetic imagery both paid special attention to slaves and slavery. Among other things, when an Israelite slave was offered freedom, the slave could choose to remain with the master forever. The master then bored a hole in the slave's earlobe with an awl (Exod. 21:6), and the pierced ear signified perpetual slavery. It was this wonderful truth Bishop C. G. Moule (1841–1920) realized when he wrote these expressive lines:

My Master, lead me to Thy door,
Pierce this now willing ear once more.

. . . .

And pierced ears shall hear the tone
Which tells me Thou and I are one.

Do we bear in this part of our body the marks of the Lord Jesus? What deeper spirituality would be ours if only our ears were more closely identified with the ears of Jesus! How can we expect to have tranquility of soul if we allow the rude voices of the world to enter our ears without a protest?

> Open my ears, that I may hear
> Voices of truth Thou sendest clear;
> And while the wavenotes fall on my ear,
> Everything false will disappear.[5]

Two Strings of the Eyes

We praise the Lord with the strings of our eyes when we deliberately close them to the sights that would dazzle us. John Bunyan makes Christian say of the "very grave person" in the house of the interpreter, "He bore his great commission in his look."[6] Do we? Have our features the evidence of a peerless unearthly communion? Have our eyes that heavenly radiance which comes through always gazing into the mirror of Scripture? Do we present the lovely face of our adorable Lord? Job speaks of making a covenant with his eyes (31:1). Have we the same fixed determination to guard our eyes?

Our eyes are the windows of the soul. Tennyson speaks about being "a part of all that I have seen." Paul reminds us that "Beholding . . . [we] are changed into the same image," (2 Cor. 3:18 KJV). Vision determines character. May grace be ours to accustom our eyes to gaze upon the lovely things of life! If, like Isaiah, we can confess, "Mine eyes have seen the King, the LORD of Hosts," (6:5 KJV) then with the responsive strings of our eyes we shall ever be found praising Him.

One String of the Tongue

One of the chief strings of the human heart is the tongue.

With the tongue we praise our Lord and Father, . . . Out of the same mouth come praise and cursing. . . . this should not be. Can both fresh water and salt water flow from the same spring? (James 3:9–11 NIV)

If ours is to be the tongue of the wise, which Solomon says is health, then we must pray:

Set a guard over my mouth, O LORD;
keep watch over the door of my lips.
(Ps. 141:3 NIV)

Take my lips, and let them be
Filled with messages from Thee.[7]

One String of the Heart

This tenth and last string of the instrument of the body praises the Lord when we are willing for Him to make our hearts His royal throne. Fashioning our heart, He made it a throne capable of holding only one ruler. He, and He only, must reign. It is thus we pray:

Take my heart, it is Thine own
It shall be Thy royal throne.[8]

Recognizing that in Scripture the heart signifies all our inward powers, affections, thoughts, and purposes, we understand what David meant when he wrote:

I give you thanks, O LORD, with all my heart;
I will sing your praises before the gods.
(Ps. 138:1 NLT)

He is wholehearted in his praises—all powers of heart, mind, and will combine to adore the Lord whom the psalmist dearly loves. The union of all inward possessions, as well as the actions of our outer lives, must ever be related to the utterance of the lips.

The intriguing title of one of Oswald Chambers' (1874–1917) volumes is *My Utmost for His Highest*,[9] and it is only as the Highest has our utmost that we have His constant smile and benediction. A mystic, who understood this truth of complete dedication of all that we have, taught us to pray:

> Lord Jesus, by Thy wounded feet, O guide my feet aright,
> Lord Jesus, by Thy wounded hands, O keep my hands from wrong,
> Lord Jesus, by Thy parched lips, O curb my cruel tongue,
> Lord Jesus, by Thy closed eyes, O guard my inward sight.
> Lord Jesus, by Thy thorn-crowned brow, O purify my mind.
> Lord Jesus, by Thy pierced heart, O knit my heart to Thine.

Tuning the Instrument

Instruments of any kind can produce no harmony if they are out of tune or if they have lost or damaged strings. This is why we have tuners. If your piano, for example, is out of tune, you send for the tuner to work on your flat instrument. What is the meaning of the dull, unharmonious, monotonous noises that the tuner evokes as he works? "Why," you say, "he is tuning my piano and bringing it back to concert pitch!" Exactly so. The Holy Spirit is the heavenly tuner, laboring to adjust the flat instrument of our lives to the will of God. He is never satisfied unless we are at heavenly concert pitch. Well might we pray:

> O may my heart in tune be found,
> Like David's harp of solemn sound![10]

David writes of having a "new song" in his mouth that others will see and fear (Ps. 40:3 NIV). How can we see a song? The rhythm of a rectified life is something that can be seen as well as heard. Are those around us charmed as they see as well as hear the new song that both lips and life must echo forth?

Perhaps there is discord within the heart simply because two or three strings need to be tightened. There are a few chords at strong tensions, consequently requiring the master's touch. Your talents are few, your education meager, your personality lacking in charm and appeal. Why should God trouble with such a nonentity? The lesson all of us have to learn, however, is that it is not so much what we may have, naturally or acquired, but what God is able to impart that counts. This is why He is able to produce the sweetest music out of the lowliest lives.

Looking upon all our faculties as strings of an instrument, can we say that everything is at the disposal of the heavenly musician? Is every part of our entire life adjusted to the will of God? Have we the assurance that there is no discord within and without? If so, then harmoniously blending with divine resources, the greatest of all musicians will be able to make "life, death, and the vast forever / One grand, sweet song."[11]

'Twas battered and scarred, and the auctioneer
thought it scarcely worth his while
to waste much time on the old violin,
but held it up with a smile.

"What am I bid, good folk, " he cried,
"Who'll start bidding for me?"
"A dollar, a dollar"; then "Two. Only two?
Two dollars, and who'll make it three?

"Three dollars, once; three dollars, twice;
going for three . . . but no!"
From the room far back, a gray-haired man
came forward and picked up the bow;

then wiping the dust from the old violin,
and tightening the loosened strings,
he played a melody, pure and sweet,
as a caroling angel sings.

The music ceased, and the auctioneer,
with a voice that was quiet and low,
said, "What am I bid for the old violin?"
and he held it up with the bow.

"A thousand dollars, and who'll make it two?
Two thousand, and who'll make it three?
Three thousand, once; three thousand, twice;
and going, and gone," said he.

The people cheered, but some of them cried,
"We do not quite understand.
What changed its worth?" Swift came the reply,
"The touch of the master's hand."[12]

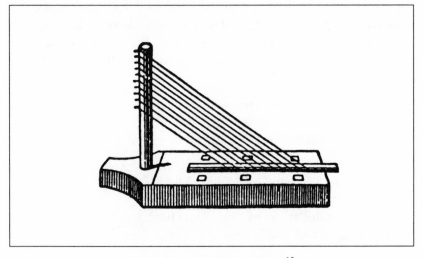

An Instrument of Ten Strings[13]
Figure 13.1 from the Sephardic Jews of Spain

14

Nebuchadnezzar's Orchestra

They spoke up and said to King Nebuchadnezzar, "O king, live forever! You, O king, gave an order that everyone who hears the horn, pipe, zither, lyre, psaltery, bagpipe, and all types of instruments must fall down and worship the golden statue, and whoever does not fall down and worship shall be thrown into a burning fiery furnace. There are certain Jews whom you appointed to administer the province of Babylon, Shadrach, Meshach, and Abed-nego; those men pay no heed to you, O king; they do not serve your god or worship the statue of gold that you have set up."
—Daniel 3:9–12 (NJPS)

THE TEXT ITSELF is musical. Like a refrain in the third chapter of Daniel, the litany of the instruments is repeated four times—the horn, pipe, zither, lyre, psaltery, bagpipe, and all other types of instruments.

Nebuchadnezzar's band played before the gates of the crowded city of Babylon (2500 B.C.). The beautiful hanging gardens, one of the seven wonders of the ancient world, were in full bloom. The birds were singing. It was a day of celebration. The king had erected a ninety-foot golden statute before which all were commanded to pay homage. Toward the end of the day, the music stopped. Three Hebrew young men had refused to bow down before the image. Enraged, the king ordered Shadrach, Meshach, and Abednego thrown into the fiery furnace. Thousands of captive Jews began to pray. They knew the king had burned men before (Jeremiah 29:22). The fire was stoked, and the soldiers were consumed by the intense heat as they threw the Hebrews into the furnace. The king gazed into the furnace and exclaimed!

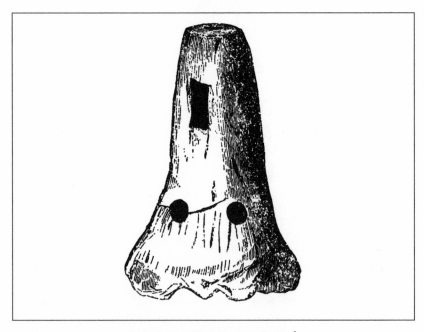

Baked Clay Pipe from Babylon[1]
Figure 14.1 from *Birs-i-Nimrod,* presented by Willock
to the Museum of the Royal Asiatic Society

Then Nebuchadnezzar the king was astonied, and rose up in haste, and spake, and said unto his counsellors, Did not we cast three men bound into the midst of the fire? They answered and said unto the king, True, O king.

He answered and said, Lo, I see four men loose, walking in the midst of the fire, and they have no hurt; and the form of the fourth is like the Son of God.

Then Nebuchadnezzar came near to the mouth of the burning fiery furnace, and spake, and said, Shadrach, Meshach, and Abed-nego, ye servants of the most high God, come forth, and come hither. Then Shadrach, Meshach, and Abed-nego, came forth of the midst of the fire.

And the princes, governors, and captains, and the king's counsellors, being gathered together, saw these men, upon whose bodies the fire had no power, nor was an hair of their head singed, neither were their coats changed, nor the smell of fire had passed on them.

Then Nebuchadnezzar spake, and said, Blessed be the God of Shadrach, Meshach, and Abed-nego, who hath sent his angel, and delivered his servants that trusted in him, and have changed the king's word, and yielded their bodies, that they might not serve nor worship any god, except their own God.

Therefore I make a decree, That every people, nation, and language, which speak any thing amiss against the God of Shadrach, Meshach, and Abed-nego, shall be cut in pieces, and their houses shall be made a dunghill: because there is no other God that can deliver after this sort.

Then the king promoted Shadrach, Meshach, and Abed-nego, in the province of Babylon. (Dan. 3:24–30 KJV)

15

Beethoven and the Blind Girl

WHILE OUT FOR AN EVENING WALK in Bonn, Germany, Ludwig von Beethoven (1770–1827) heard the sound of a piano coming through the open window of a house. As a musician, always ready to listen to music, he stopped and recognized that what was being played was music he himself had written. He quickly detected that the person playing could not play well, and was interested to hear a woman's voice exclaim in despair, "Oh, it's no use. The music is so, so beautiful, but I can't play it, and I shall only ruin it if I try any longer."

Beethoven was sorry for the person whose words were spoken with such sadness, and tapping on the door, he asked, "May I come in and play it for you?" He found two women in the room who did not know him; he quickly realized the younger of the two sitting at the piano was blind. Kindly, Beethoven took her place and played the music he had written, as only he could play it.

"Oh, that is wonderful, wonderful," exclaimed the blind girl. "Do go on, play something else."

Moonlight, which of course the blind girl could not see, was streaming through the open window as the great master's fingers moved effortlessly across the keys. Soon a wonderful melody filled the room. The two women listened enraptured as Beethoven blended the soft night with the sympathy he felt for the sightless girl.

Hurrying home he sat down and recaptured the music he had played to the blind girl and her companion. What he wrote became known to the world as the "Moonlight Sonata." Had Beethoven not stopped to play for the blind girl that night, manifesting sympathy and kindness as he did, the world might never have received such a remarkable composition. With sympathy born of his own hearing loss, he gave the girl what he could, and God gave him still more—this, in turn, Beethoven gave the world.

Notes

Foreword

1. Source unknown.

2. Herbert Lockyer Sr., "The Bible Student's Companion," *The Witness* (May 1962): n.p.

3. Martin Luther, "Foreword" in *Wittenberg Gesangbuch* (n.p., 1524), n.p.

Chapter 1, Ancient Music

1. Don E. Saliers, "Singing Our Lives" in *Practicing Our Faith: A Way of Life for a Searching People* (ed. Dorothy C. Bass; San Francisco: Jossey-Bass, 1997), 180.

2. A. D. Kilmer, "World's Oldest Musical Notation Deciphered on Cuneiform Tablet," *BAR* VI, 5 (1980): 14–25.

3. Carl Engel, *The Music of the Most Ancient Nations* (London: Reeves, 1929), 302–3.

Chapter 2, Songs of Moses

1. Carl Engel, *The Music of the Most Ancient Nations* (London: Reeves, 1929), 220.

2. Samuel Stennett (1727–1795), *On Jordan's Stormy Banks.*

Chapter 3, Songs of Deborah and Hannah

1. Wendy M. Wright, "Sing to the Lord a New Song," *Weavings* VI, 5 (1991), 7–17.
2. Don E. Saliers, "Singing Our Lives" in *Practicing Our Faith: A Way of Life for a Searching People* (ed. Dorothy C. Bass; San Francisco: Jossey-Bass, 1997), 182.
3. J. Cheryl Exum, "Judges," in *Harper's Bible Commentary* (ed. James L. Mays; San Francisco: Harper & Row, 1988), 251.
4. Wright.
5. Robert L. Cohen, "1 Samuel," in *Harper's Bible Commentary* (ed. James L. Mays; San Francisco: Harper & Row, 1988), 269.
6. Walter Brueggemann, *First and Second Samuel* (Interpretation; Louisville, Ky.: John Knox, 1990), 12.
7. Ibid.
8. Carl Engel, *The Music of the Most Ancient Nations* (London: Reeves, 1929), 77.

Chapter 5, Instruments of Praise

1. John Stainer, *The Music of the Bible* (London: Novello, 1914), 23–24.
2. Charles H. Spurgeon, "Psalm 92," in *Psalms 58–110* (vol. 2 of *The Treasury of David Containing an Original Exposition of the Book of Psalms;* repr. Peabody, Mass.: Hendrickson, 1988), 117.
3. James Millar, "Music," *ISBE* 3:2094–2101.
4. Ibid.
5. John Stainer, *The Music of the Bible* (London: Novello, 1914), 155.
6. Lee G. Olson, "Music and the Musical Instruments of the Bible," *Zondervan's Pictorial Bible Encyclopedia,* 4:562–66.
7. Adam Clarke, "Job 21," in *Clarke's Commentary* 1 (6 vols.; New York: Mason & Lane, 1837), 376.
8. Carl Engel, *The Music of the Most Ancient Nations* (London: Reeves, 1929), 224.

Chapter 6, The Significance of Hebrew Poetry

1. Peter Fitz, "History of Jewish Music," University of Baltimore, April 11, 2000, http://www.ubmail.ubalt.edu/~pfitz/play/ref/histjew.htm (accessed April 16, 2004).

2. Wayne A. Meeks, "Introduction to the HarperCollins Study Bible," *The HarperCollins Study Bible, New Revised Standard Version* (New York: HarperCollins, 1989), xviii.

Chapter 7, Songs of King David

1. Wadis are dried river beds in the Holy Lands that flood with torrential rushing waters in times of heavy rains and quickly become impassable.

2. Carl Engel, *The Music of the Most Ancient Nations* (London: Reeves, 1929), 225–26.

Chapter 8, The Psalter: Hymnbook of the Hebrews

1. John Calvin, *Commentary on the Book of Psalms* 1 (Edinburgh: Calvin Translation Society, 1845), xxxviii–xxxix.

2. Ibid., xxxvi.

3. John Calvin, *Commentary on the Book of Psalms* 1 (Grand Rapids, Mich.: Eerdmans, 1949), xxxvii.

4. Credit is given here to the Rev. Dr. Gary W. Klingsporn, Teaching Minister, Colonial Church of Edina, Minnesota, who teaches and lectures frequently on the book of Psalms. He generously made available a wealth of unpublished lecture notes to supplement the original research and compilation of Dr. Herbert Lockyer Sr. This material is used by permission.

5. Martin Luther, "Preface to the Psalter" in *Luther's Works* 35 (Philadelphia: Fortress, 1960), 255–56.

Chapter 9, Songs of Isaiah

1. Sir. 48:22b–25 JB.
2. F. C. Jennings, *Studies in Isaiah* (Neptune, N.J.: Loizeaux Brothers, n.d.), n.p.
3. Walter Brueggeman, *Texts for Preaching*, (Louisville, Ky.: Westminster John Knox, 1995), 21.
4. Carl Engel, *The Music of the Most Ancient Nations* (London: Reeves, 1929), 242.

Chapter 10, King Solomon's Song of Songs

1. Marcia Falk, "Song of Songs," in *Harper's Bible Commentary* (ed. James L. Mays; San Francisco: Harper & Row, 1988), 526.

Chapter 11, Songs of the New Testament

1. Robert E. Webber, "Elements of New Testament Worship," in *The Biblical Foundations of Christian Worship* (ed. Robert E. Webber; vol. 1 of *The Complete Library of Christian Worship*, ed. Robert E. Webber; Nashville, Tenn.: Star Song, 1993), 106–10.
2. Text: Reginald Heber, 1783–1826, alt.
3. Richard L. Jeske, *Revelation: Images of Hope* (Inspire Bible Study Series; Minneapolis: Augsburg Fortress, 1998), 28.
4. Matthew Henry, *Acts to Revelation* (vol. 6 of *Matthew Henry's Commentary on the Whole Bible*; repr. Peabody, Mass.: Hendrickson, 1992), 920–21.

Chapter 12, The Birth of the Modern Hymn

1. Pliny of Rome (A.D. 67–113).
2. Tertullian (A.D. 155–220), from his essay on marriage.
3. John Stainer, *The Music of the Bible* (London: Novello, 1914), 31–32.

4. H. T. McElrath, "Music in Christianity," *The Perennial Dictionary of World Religions* (ed. Keith Crim; San Francisco: Harper & Row, 1981), 505.

5. J. B. MacMillan, "Christian Music," *The New International Dictionary of the Christian Church* (ed. J. D. Douglas; Grand Rapids, Mich.: Zondervan, 1974), 689.

6. W. S. Reid, "John Calvin," *The New International Dictionary of the Christian Church* (ed. J. D. Douglas; Grand Rapids, Mich.: Zondervan, 1974), 179.

Chapter 13, Instrument of Ten Strings

1. Herbert Lockyer Sr., "Instrument of Ten Strings," sermon preached on WMBI, 1924.

2. Ibid.

3. Frances R. Havergal, "Take My Life and Let It Be," 1874.

4. Ibid.

5. Clara H. Fiske Scott, "Open My Eyes, That I May See," in *Best Hymns No. 2* (ed. Elisha A. Hoffman and Harold F. Sayles; Chicago, Ill.: Evangelical Publishing Company, 1895).

6. John Bunyan, *Pilgrim's Progress.*

7. Havergal.

8. Ibid.

9. Oswald Chambers, *My Utmost for His Highest* (New York: Dodd Mead, 1937).

10. Isaac Watts, "Sweet Is the Work, My God, My King," 1917.

11. Myra Brooks Welch, "The Touch of the Master's Hand," tract (Grand Rapids, Mich.: Kregel, 1946).

12. Charles Kingsley, "A Farewell," in *A Victorian Anthology* (ed. Edmund Clarence Stedman; Cambridge: Riverside, 1895).

13. John Stainer, *The Music of the Bible* (London: Novello, 1914), 15.

Chapter 14, Nebuchadnezzar's Orchestra

1. Carl Engel, *The Music of the Most Ancient Nations* (London: Reeves, 1929), 75–76.

APPENDICES

■   ■   ■

A

Psalms That Mention Song or Singing (KJV)

Psalm	Scripture
I . . . will **sing** praise to the name of the LORD most high.	7:17
I will **sing** praise to thy name, O thou most High.	9:2
Sing praises to the LORD.	9:11
I will **sing** unto the LORD, because he hath dealt bountifully with me.	13:6
Sing praises unto thy name.	18:49
So will we **sing** and praise thy power.	21:13
I will **sing**, yea, I will **sing** praises unto the LORD.	27:6
And with my **song** will I praise him.	28:7
Sing unto the LORD, O ye saints of his.	30:4
To the end that my glory may **sing** praise to thee, and not be silent.	30:12
Thou shalt compass me about with **songs** of deliverance.	32:7
Sing unto him with the psaltery.	33:2
Sing unto him a new **song**.	33:3
And he hath put a new **song** in my mouth.	40:3
In the night his **song** shall be with me.	42:8
Sing praises to God, **sing** praises: **sing** praises unto our King, **sing** praises.	47:6

Sing ye praises with understanding.	47:7
My tongue shall **sing** aloud of thy righteousness.	51:14
I will **sing** and give praise.	57:7
I will **sing** unto thee among the nations.	57:9
But I will **sing** of thy power; yea, I will **sing** aloud of thy mercy.	59:16
Unto thee, O my strength, will I **sing.**	59:17
So will I **sing** praise unto thy name for ever.	61:8
They shout for joy, they also **sing**.	65:13
Sing forth the honour of his name.	66:2
All the earth . . . shall **sing** unto thee; they shall **sing** to thy name.	66:4
O let the nations be glad and **sing** for joy.	67:4
Sing unto God, **sing** praises to his name.	68:4
The **singers** went before, the players on instruments followed after.	68:25
Sing unto God . . . O **sing** praises unto the Lord	68:32
I was the **song** of the drunkards.	69:12
I will praise the name of God with a **song.**	69:30
Unto thee will I **sing** with the harp.	71:22
My lips shall greatly rejoice when I **sing** unto thee.	71:23
I will **sing** praises to the God of Jacob.	75:9
I call to remembrance my **song** in the night.	77:6
Sing aloud unto God our strength.	81:1
As well the **singers** as the players on instruments shall be there.	87:7
I will **sing** of the mercies of the LORD.	89:1
And to **sing** praises unto thy name, O most High.	92:1
O come, let us **sing** unto the LORD.	95:1
Make a joyful noise unto him with psalms.	95:2

O **sing** unto the LORD a new **song: sing** unto the LORD,   96:1
all the earth.

Sing unto the LORD, bless his name.   96:2

O **sing** unto the LORD a new **song.**   98:1

Rejoice, and **sing** praise.   98:4

Sing unto the LORD with . . . the voice of a psalm.   98:5

Come before his presence with **singing.**   100:2

I will **sing** of mercy and judgment: unto thee, O LORD,   101:1
will I **sing.**

The fowls of the heaven have their habitation, which   104:12
sing among the branches.

I will **sing** unto the LORD . . . I will **sing** praise to my   104:33
God.

Sing unto him, **sing** psalms unto him.   105:2

I will **sing** and give praise.   108:1

I will **sing** praises unto thee among the nations.   108:3

The LORD is my strength and **song,** and is become my   118:14
salvation.

Thy statutes have been my **songs** in the house of my   119:54
pilgrimage.

Then was our mouth filled with laughter, and our   126:2
tongue with **singing.**

Sing praises unto his name; for it is pleasant.   135:3

They . . . required of us a **song** . . . saying, **Sing** us one of   137:3
the **songs** of Zion.

How shall we **sing** the LORD's **song?**   137:4

I **sing** praise unto thee.   138:1

Yea, they shall **sing** in the ways of the LORD.   138:5

I will **sing** a new **song** unto thee, O God . . . will I **sing**   144:9
praises unto thee.

I will **sing** praises unto my God while I have any being.   146:2

It is good to **sing** praises unto our God.	147:1
Sing unto the LORD with thanksgiving; **sing** praise upon the harp.	147:7
Sing unto the LORD a new **song.**	149:1
Let them **sing** praises unto him.	149:3
Let them **sing** aloud upon their beds.	149:5

B

Well-Known Songs
and Hymns of the Bible

Singers and Songs	Scripture
Moses and Miriam after leading Israel through the Red Sea	Exod. 15:1–18, 21
Moses before his translation to heaven	Deut. 32:1–43
Israel at the well at Beer en route to the promised land	Num. 21:17–18
Deborah and Barak after their victory over Sisera	Judg. 5:1–31
Hannah during the dedication of her son Samuel	1 Sam. 2:1–10
Israelite women to celebrate David's victory over Goliath	1 Sam. 18:6–7
Levitical choirs at the temple dedication	2 Chr. 5:12–14
Jehoshaphat's marching choir to lead the soldiers into battle	2 Chr. 20:21–22
Levitical choirs at Hezekiah's rededication of the temple	2 Chr. 29:25–30
Israelites in their song book	Pss. 1–150
Solomon and his bride	Song 1–8
Mary upon learning of the future virgin birth	Luke 1:46–55

Zacharias at the circumcision of his son John the Baptist	Luke 1:68–79
Angels at Jesus' birth	Luke 2:13–14
Jesus and the disciples in the upper room	Matt. 26:30
Paul and Silas while in a Philippian jail at midnight	Acts 16:25
Believers to praise God	Eph. 5:19, Col. 3:16
All believers to glorify Christ in heaven	Rev. 5:9–10
Choir of 144,000 to the Lamb	Rev. 14:1–3
Saints after their victory in tribulation	Rev. 15:2–4

C

Songs of the Bible, Mentioned Only by Name

NUMEROUS SONGS OR TUNES are mentioned in the Bible but were never recorded for the people of God. Listed here are the Scriptures references to songs lost to our knowledge unless some future archeologist unearths a treasure trove of as yet undiscovered findings.

Song	Scripture
Songs of the Morning	Judg. 5:12
Songs in the Night	Job 35:10 Pss. 42:8; 77:6 Isa. 30:29
Singing in Bed	Ps. 149:5
Songs of Joy	1 Sam. 18:6 Pss. 65:8; 71:23; 100:2; 126:2
Songs of Thanksgiving	Neh. 12:8 Jer. 30:19 John 2:9
Songs of Deliverance	Ps. 32:7
Song for the Sabbath Day	Ps. 92:1–15
New Songs	Pss. 33:3; 40:3; 144:9; 149:1 Rev. 14:3

Spiritual Songs	Eph. 5:19
	Col. 3:16
Love Song	Isa. 5:1
Wedding Songs	Pss. 45:1–17; 78:63
Song of the Widow	Job 29:14
Song of Fools	Eccl. 7:5
Song of Mockery	Lam. 3:14
Noisy Songs	Ezek. 26:13
	Amos 5:23
Ruthless Songs	Isa. 25:5
Song of the Drunkards	Ps. 69:12
Song of the Prostitute	Isa. 23:9
Song of the Forest	Ps. 96:12
Song of the Trees	1 Chr. 16:23
Song of the Mountains	Isa. 44:23; 49:13
Song of the Stars	Job 38:7
Lost Songs	1 Kgs. 4:32

D

References in the Bible to Instruments (KJV)

Bell	Scripture
and **bells** of gold between them round about	Exod. 28:33
A golden **bell** and a pomegranate, a golden **bell** and a pomegranate	Exod. 28:34
made **bells** of pure gold, and put the **bells** between the pomegranates	Exod. 39:25
A **bell** and a pomegranate, a **bell** and a pomegranate, round	Exod. 39:26
In that day shall there be upon the **bells** of the horses	Zech. 14:20

Cornet	Scripture
even on harps, and on psalteries, and on timbrels, and on **cornets**	2 Sam. 6:5
with shouting, and with sound of the **cornet,** and with trumpets	1 Chr. 15:28
and with shouting, and with trumpets, and with **cornets**	2 Chr. 15:14

With trumpets and sound of **cornet** make a joyful noise	Ps. 98:6
That at what time ye hear the sound of the **cornet,** flute	Dan. 3:5
when all the people heard the sound of the **cornet,** flute	Dan. 3:7
that every man that shall hear the sound of the **cornet,** flute	Dan. 3:10
Now if ye be ready that at what time ye hear the sound of the **cornet,** flute	Dan. 3:15
Blow ye the **cornet** in Gibeah, and the trumpet in Ramah	Hos. 5:8

Cymbals	**Scripture**
and on timbrels, and on cornets, and on **cymbals**	2 Sam. 6:5
with **cymbals**, and with trumpets	1 Chr. 13:8
harps and **cymbals**, sounding, by lifting up the voice with joy	1 Chr. 15:16
were appointed to sound with **cymbals** of brass	1 Chr. 15:19
with **cymbals**, making a noise with psalteries and harps	1 Chr. 15:28
but Asaph made a sound with **cymbals**	1 Chr. 16:5
with trumpets and **cymbals** for those that should make a sound	1 Chr. 16:42
who should prophesy with harps, with psalteries, and with **cymbals**	1 Chr. 25:1
for song in the house of the LORD, with **cymbals**	1 Chr. 25:6

being arrayed in white linen, having **cymbals**	2 Chr. 5:12
when they lifted up their voice with the trumpets and **cymbals**	2 Chr. 5:13
he set the Levites in the house of the LORD with **cymbals**	2 Chr. 29:25
the Levites the sons of Asaph with **cymbals**	Ezra 3:10
with singing, with **cymbals**, psalteries, and with harps	Neh. 12:27
Praise him upon the loud **cymbals**	Ps. 150:5
praise him upon the high sounding **cymbals**	Ps. 150:5
I am become as sounding brass, or a tinkling **cymbal**	1 Cor. 13:1

Dulcimer	**Scripture**
sackbut, psaltery, **dulcimer**, and all kinds of music	Dan. 3:5
sackbut, psaltery, and **dulcimer**, and all kinds of music	Dan. 3:10
sackbut, psaltery, and **dulcimer**, and all kinds of music	Dan. 3:15

Flute	**Scripture**
That at what time ye hear the sound of the cornet, **flute**, harp	Dan. 3:5
when all the people heard the sound of the cornet, **flute**, harp	Dan. 3:7
every man that shall hear the sound of the cornet, **flute**, harp	Dan. 3:10
at what time ye hear the sound of the cornet, **flute**, harp	Dan. 3:15

Harp	Scripture
he was the father of all such as handle the **harp**	Gen. 4:21
with mirth, and with songs, with tabret, and with **harp**	Gen. 31:27
with a psaltery, and a tabret, and a pipe, and a **harp**, before them	1 Sam. 10:5
who is a cunning player on an **harp**	1 Sam. 16:16
that David took an **harp**, and played with his hand	1 Sam. 16:23
all manner of instruments made of fir wood, even on **harps**	2 Sam. 6:5
and for the king's house, **harps** also and psalteries for singers	1 Kgs. 10:12
with singing, and with **harps**, and with psalteries, and with timbrels	1 Chr. 13:8
to be the singers with instruments of music, psalteries and **harps**	1 Chr. 15:16
and Azaziah, with **harps** on the Sheminith to excel	1 Chr. 15:21
making a noise with psalteries and **harps**	1 Chr. 15:28
and Jeiel with psalteries and with **harps**	1 Chr. 16:5
who should prophesy with **harps**, with psalteries, and with cymbals	1 Chr. 25:1
sons of Jeduthun, who prophesied with a **harp**	1 Chr. 25:3
with cymbals, psalteries, and **harps**	1 Chr. 25:6
having cymbals and psalteries and **harps**	2 Chr. 5:12
and **harps** and psalteries for singers	2 Chr. 9:11

they came to Jerusalem with psalteries and **harps** and trumpets ·	2 Chr. 20:28
with psalteries, and with **harps**, according to the commandment of David	2 Chr. 29:25
and with singing, with cymbals, psalteries, and with **harps**.	Neh. 12:27
They take the timbrel and **harp**	Job 21:12
My **harp** also is turned to mourning	Job 30:31
Praise the LORD with **harp**	Ps. 33:2
upon the **harp** will I praise thee	Ps. 43:4
I will open my dark saying upon the **harp**	Ps. 49:4
awake, psaltery and **harp**	Ps. 57:8
unto thee will I sing with the **harp**	Ps. 71:22
bring hither the timbrel, the pleasant **harp** with the psaltery	Ps. 81:2
upon the **harp** with a solemn sound	Ps. 92:3
Sing unto the LORD with the **harp**	Ps. 98:5
with the **harp**, and the voice of a psalm	Ps. 98:5
Awake, psaltery and **harp**	Ps. 108:2
We hanged our **harps** upon the willows in the midst thereof	Ps. 137:2
sing praise upon the **harp** unto our God	Ps. 147:7
let them sing praises unto him with the timbrel and **harp**	Ps. 149:3
praise him with the psaltery and **harp**	Ps. 150:3
And the **harp**, and the viol, the tabret, and pipe, and wine, are in their feasts	Isa. 5:12

Wherefore my bowels shall sound like an **harp** for Moab	Isa. 16:11
Take an **harp**, go about the city, thou harlot that hast been forgotten	Isa. 23:16
the joy of the **harp** ceaseth	Isa. 24:8
it shall be with tabrets and **harps**	Isa. 30:32
and the sound of thy **harps** shall be no more heard	Ezek. 26:13
That at what time ye hear the sound of the cornet, flute, **harp**	Dan. 3:5
when all the people heard the sound of the cornet, flute, **harp**	Dan. 3:7
every man that shall hear the sound of the cornet, flute, **harp**	Dan. 3:10
ye hear the sound of the cornet, flute, **harp**, sackbut, psaltery	Dan. 3:15
whether pipe or **harp**, except they give a distinction in the sounds	1 Cor. 14:7
how shall it be known what is piped or **harp**ed	1 Cor. 14:7
having every one of them **harps**, and golden vials full of odours	Rev. 5:8
and I heard the voice of **harp**ers **harp**ing with their **harps**	Rev. 14:2
stand on the sea of glass, having the **harps** of God.	Rev. 15:2
And the voice of **harp**ers, and musicians, and of pipers	Rev. 18:22

Horn	Scripture
And seven priests shall bear before the ark seven trumpets of rams' **horns**	Josh. 6:4
when they make a long blast with the ram's **horn**, and when ye hear the sound	Josh. 6:5
bear seven trumpets of rams' **horns** before the ark of the LORD	Josh. 6:6
bearing the seven trumpets of rams' **horns** passed on before the LORD	Josh. 6:8
priests bearing seven trumpets of rams' **horns** before the ark of the LORD	Josh. 6:13

Organ	Scripture
the father of all such as handle the harp and **organ**	Gen. 4:21
and rejoice at the sound of the **organ**	Job 21:12
my **organ** into the voice of them that weep	Job 30:31
praise him with stringed instruments and **organs**	Ps. 150:4

Pipe	Scripture
and a **pipe**, and a harp, before them; and they shall prophesy	1 Sam. 10:5
the people **piped** with **pipes**, and rejoiced with great joy	1 Kgs. 1:40
the harp, and the viol, the tabret, and **pipe**, and wine, are in their feasts	Isa. 5:12
as when one goeth with a **pipe** to come into the mountain of the LORD	Isa. 30:29

Therefore mine heart shall sound for Moab like **pipes**	Jer. 48:36
mine heart shall sound like **pipes** for the men of Kir-heres	Jer. 48:36
the workmanship of thy tabrets and of thy **pipes** was prepared in thee	Ezek. 28:13
We have **piped** unto you, and ye have not danced	Matt. 11:17
We have **piped** unto you, and ye have not danced	Luke 7:32
even things without life giving sound, whether **pipe** or harp	1 Cor. 14:7
the voice of harpers, and musicians, and of **pipers**	Rev. 18:22

Psaltery	**Scripture**
prophets coming down from the high place with a **psaltery**	1 Sam. 10:5
and on **psalteries**, and on timbrels, and on cornets, and on cymbals	2 Sam. 6:5
and for the king's house, harps also and **psalteries** for singers	1 Kgs. 10:12
and with **psalteries**, and with timbrels, and with cymbals	1 Chr. 13:8
psalteries and harps and cymbals	1 Chr. 15:16
and Benaiah, with **psalteries** on Alamoth	1 Chr. 15:20
making a noise with **psalteries** and harps	1 Chr. 15:28
and Jeiel with **psalteries** and with harps	1 Chr. 16:5
who should prophesy with harps, with **psalteries**	1 Chr. 25:1

with cymbals, **psalteries**, and harps	1 Chr. 25:6
having cymbals and **psalteries** and harps	2 Chr. 5:12
and to the king's palace, and harps and **psalteries** for singers	2 Chr. 9:11
And they came to Jerusalem with **psalteries** and harps	2 Chr. 20:28
with **psalteries**, and with harps	2 Chr. 29:25
and with singing, with cymbals, **psalteries**, and with harps	Neh. 12:27
sing unto him with the **psaltery** and an instrument of ten strings	Ps. 33:2
Awake up, my glory; awake, **psaltery** and harp	Ps. 57:8
I will also praise thee with the **psaltery**	Ps. 71:22
the pleasant harp with the **psaltery**	Ps. 81:2
and upon the **psaltery**; upon the harp with a solemn sound	Ps. 92:3
Awake, **psaltery** and harp	Ps. 108:2
upon a **psaltery** and an instrument of ten strings will I sing praises unto thee	Ps. 144:9
praise him with the **psaltery** and harp	Ps. 150:3
psaltery, dulcimer, and all kinds of music, ye fall down	Dan. 3:5
psaltery, and all kinds of music, all the people	Dan. 3:7
psaltery, and dulcimer, and all kinds of music	Dan. 3:10
psaltery, and dulcimer, and all kinds of music	Dan. 3:15

Sackbut	Scripture
harp, **sackbut**, psaltery, dulcimer, and all kinds of music	Dan. 3:5
all the people heard the sound of the cornet, flute, harp, **sackbut,** psaltery	Dan. 3:7
the sound of the cornet, flute, harp, **sackbut,** psaltery, and dulcimer	Dan. 3:10
ye hear the sound of the cornet, flute, harp, **sackbut,** psaltery	Dan. 3:15

Tabret	Scripture
sent thee away with mirth, and with songs, with **tabret**	Gen. 31:27
prophets coming down from the high place with a psaltery, and a **tabret**	1 Sam. 10:5
dancing, to meet king Saul, with **tabrets,** with joy	1 Sam. 18:6
aforetime I was as a **tabret**	Job 17:6
the **tabret**, and pipe, and wine, are in their feasts	Isa. 5:12
The mirth of **tabrets** ceaseth	Isa. 24:8
it shall be with **tabrets** and harps	Isa. 30:32
thou shalt again be adorned with thy **tabrets**	Jer. 31:4
the workmanship of thy **tabrets** and of thy pipes	Ezek. 28:13

Timbrel	Scripture
Miriam . . . took a **timbrel** in her hand	Exod. 15:20

all the women went out after her with **timbrels** and with dances	Exod. 15:20
his daughter came out to meet him with **timbrels** and with dances	Judg. 11:34
and on **timbrels**, and on cornets, and on cymbals	2 Sam. 6:5
and with **timbrels**, and with cymbals, and with trumpets	1 Chr. 13:8
They take the **timbrel** and harp, and rejoice	Job 21:12
among them were the damsels playing with **timbrels**	Ps. 68:25
bring hither the **timbrel**, the pleasant harp with the psaltery	Ps. 81:2
let them sing praises unto him with the **timbrel** and harp	Ps. 149:3
Praise him with the **timbrel** and dance	Ps. 150:4

Trumpet	**Scripture**
when the **trumpet** soundeth long, they shall come up to the mount	Exod. 19:13
the voice of the **trumpet** exceeding loud	Exod. 19:16
when the voice of the **trumpet** sounded long	Exod. 19:19
the noise of the **trumpet**, and the mountain smoking	Exod. 20:18
a memorial of blowing of **trumpets**, an holy convocation	Lev. 23:24
Then shalt thou cause the **trumpet** of the jubile to sound	Lev. 25:9

shall ye make the **trumpet** sound throughout all your land	Lev. 25:9
Make thee two **trumpets of silver**; of a whole piece	Num. 10:2
they blow but with one **trumpet**, then the princes	Num. 10:4
blow with the **trumpets**; and they shall be to you for an ordinance	Num. 10:8
then ye shall blow an alarm with the **trumpets**	Num. 10:9
ye shall blow with the **trumpets** over your burnt offerings	Num. 10:10
it is a day of blowing the **trumpets** unto you.	Num. 29:1
with the holy instruments, and the **trumpets** to blow in his hand	Num. 31:6
seven priests shall bear before the ark seven **trumpets** of rams' horns	Josh. 6:4
the priests shall blow with the **trumpets**	Josh. 6:4
when ye hear the sound of the **trumpet**, all the people shall shout	Josh. 6:5
let seven priests bear seven **trumpets** of rams' horns	Josh. 6:6
that the seven priests bearing the seven **trumpets** of rams' horns passed on	Josh. 6:8
blew with the **trumpets**	Josh. 6:8
priests that blew with the **trumpets**, and the rearward came after the ark	Josh. 6:9
the priests going on, and blowing with the **trumpets**	Josh. 6:9

seven priests bearing seven **trumpets** of rams' horns before the ark	Josh. 6:13
blew with the **trumpets**	Josh. 6:13
blowing with the **trumpets**	Josh. 6:13
when the priests blew with the **trumpets**	Josh. 6:16
priests blew with the **trumpets**	Josh. 6:20
people heard the sound of the **trumpet**, and the people shouted	Josh. 6:20
he blew a **trumpet** in the mountain of Ephraim	Judg. 3:27
he blew a **trumpet**; and Abiezer was gathered after him	Judg. 6:34
people took victuals in their hand, and their **trumpets**	Judg. 7:8
he put a **trumpet** in every man's hand, with empty pitchers	Judg. 7:16
When I blow with a **trumpet**, I and all that are with me	Judg. 7:18
blow ye the **trumpets** also on every side of all the camp	Judg. 7:18
they blew the **trumpets**, and brake the pitchers	Judg. 7:19
three companies blew the **trumpets**, and brake the pitchers	Judg. 7:20
the **trumpets** in their right hands to blow withal	Judg. 7:20
the three hundred blew the **trumpets**	Judg. 7:22
Saul blew the **trumpet** throughout all the land	1 Sam. 13:3

Joab blew a **trumpet**, and all the people stood still	2 Sam. 2:28
ark of the LORD with shouting, and with the sound of the **trumpet**	2 Sam. 6:15
the sound of the **trumpet**, then ye shall say, Absalom reigneth	2 Sam. 15:10
Joab blew the **trumpet**, and the people returned from pursuing	2 Sam. 18:16
he blew a **trumpet**, and said, We have no part in David	2 Sam. 20:1
he blew a **trumpet**, and they retired from the city	2 Sam. 20:22
blow ye with the **trumpet**, and say, God save king Solomon	1 Kgs. 1:34
blew the **trumpet**; and all the people said, God save king Solomon	1 Kgs. 1:39
when Joab heard the sound of the **trumpet**	1 Kgs. 1:41
blew with **trumpets**, saying, Jehu is king	2 Kgs. 9:13
the princes and the **trumpeters** by the king	2 Kgs. 11:14
all the people of the land rejoiced, and blew with **trumpets**	2 Kgs. 11:14
bowls of silver, snuffers, basons, **trumpets**, any vessels of gold	2 Kgs. 12:13
and with timbrels, and with cymbals, and with **trumpets**	1 Chr. 13:8
Benaiah, and Eliezer, the priests, did blow with the **trumpets** before the ark	1 Chr. 15:24
and with **trumpets**, and with cymbals, making a noise with psalteries	1 Chr. 15:28

Benaiah ... and Jahaziel the priests with **trumpets** continually before the ark	1 Chr. 16:6
Heman and Jeduthun with **trumpets** and cymbals	1 Chr. 16:42
with them an hundred and twenty priests sounding with **trumpets**	2 Chr. 5:12
as the **trumpeters** and singers were as one	2 Chr. 5:13
when they lifted up their voice with the **trumpets** and cymbals	2 Chr. 5:13
the priests sounded **trumpets** before them, and all Israel stood	2 Chr. 7:6
his priests with sounding **trumpets** to cry alarm against you	2 Chr. 13:12
the priests sounded with the **trumpets**	2 Chr. 13:14
with shouting, and with **trumpets**, and with cornets	2 Chr. 15:14
harps and **trumpets** unto the house of the LORD	2 Chr. 20:28
and the princes and the **trumpets** by the king	2 Chr. 23:13
people of the land rejoiced, and sounded with **trumpets**	2 Chr. 23:13
instruments of David, and the priests with the **trumpets**	2 Chr. 29:26
the song of the LORD began also with the **trumpets**	2 Chr. 29:27
singers sang, and the **trumpeters** sounded	2 Chr. 29:28
they set the priests in their apparel with **trumpets**	Ezra 3:10

he that sounded the **trumpet** was by me	Neh. 4:18
hear the sound of the **trumpet**, resort ye thither unto us	Neh. 4:20
certain of the priests' sons with **trumpets**	Neh. 12:35
Elioenai, Zechariah, and Hananiah, with **trumpets**	Neh. 12:41
neither believeth he that it is the sound of the **trumpet**	Job 39:24
He saith among the **trumpets**, Ha, ha	Job 39:25
the LORD with the sound of a **trumpet**	Ps. 47:5
Blow up the **trumpet** in the new moon, in the time appointed	Ps. 81:3
With **trumpets** and sound of cornet make a joyful noise	Ps. 98:6
Praise him with the sound of the **trumpet**	Ps. 150:3
when he bloweth a **trumpet**, hear ye	Isa. 18:3
the great **trumpet** shall be blown, and they shall come	Isa. 27:13
lift up thy voice like a **trumpet**, and show my people their transgression	Isa. 58:1
Blow ye the **trumpet** in the land	Jer. 4:5
O my soul, the sound of the **trumpet**, the alarm of war	Jer. 4:19
I see the standard, and hear the sound of the **trumpet**	Jer. 4:21
flee out of the midst of Jerusalem, and blow the **trumpet**	Jer. 6:1
Hearken to the sound of the **trumpet**	Jer. 6:17

nor hear the sound of the **trumpet**, nor have hunger of bread	Jer. 42:14
blow the **trumpet** among the nations	Jer. 51:27
They have blown the **trumpet**, even to make all ready	Ezek. 7:14
he blow the **trumpet**, and warn the people	Ezek. 33:3
whosoever heareth the sound of the **trumpet**	Ezek. 33:4
He heard the sound of the **trumpet**, and took not warning	Ezek. 33:5
blow not the **trumpet**, and the people be not warned	Ezek. 33:6
Blow ye the cornet in Gibeah, and the **trumpet** in Ramah	Hos. 5:8
Set the **trumpet** to thy mouth	Hos. 8:1
Blow ye the **trumpet** in Zion, and sound an alarm in my holy mountain	Joel 2:1
Blow the **trumpet** in Zion, sanctify a fast	Joel 2:15
with shouting, and with the sound of the **trumpet**	Amos 2:2
Shall a **trumpet** be blown in the city, and the people not be afraid	Amos 3:6
A day of the **trumpet** and alarm against the fenced cities	Zeph. 1:16
the LORD God shall blow the **trumpet**	Zech. 9:14
do not sound a **trumpet** before thee, as the	Matt. 6:2
he shall send his angels with a great sound of a **trumpet**	Matt. 24:31
if the **trumpet** give an uncertain sound	1 Cor. 14:8

for the **trumpet** shall sound, and the dead shall be raised	1 Cor. 15:52
the sound of a **trumpet**, and the voice of words	Heb. 12:19
heard behind me a great voice, as of a **trumpet**	Rev. 1:10
voice which I heard was as it were of a **trumpet** talking with me	Rev. 4:1
to them were given seven **trumpets**	Rev. 8:2
seven angels which had the seven **trumpets** prepared	Rev. 8:6
the other voices of the **trumpet** of the three angels	Rev. 8:13
Saying to the sixth angel which had the **trumpet**	Rev. 9:14
and **trumpeters**, shall be heard no more at all in thee	Rev. 18:22

Viol	**Scripture**
And the harp, and the **viol**, the tabret, and pipe, and wine	Isa. 5:12
Thy pomp is brought down to the grave, and the noise of thy **viols**	Isa. 14:11
for I will not hear the melody of thy **viols**	Amos 5:23
That chant to the sound of the **viol**, and invent to themselves	Amos 6:5

E

Great Hymns and Songs of the Church

Hymn	Author
A Charge to Keep I Have	Charles Wesley
A Mighty Fortress Is Our God	Martin Luther
A Wonderful Savior Is Jesus My Lord	Fanny Crosby
Abide with Me	Henry Francis Lyte
Alas and Did My Savior Bleed	Isaac Watts
All for Jesus, All for Jesus	Mary D. James
All Hail the Power of Jesus' Name	Edward Perronet
All My Hope on God Is Founded	Joachim Neander
All People That on Earth Do Dwell	William Kethe
All the Way My Savior Leads Me	Fanny Crosby
All Things Bright and Beautiful	Cecil Francis Alexander
Am I a Soldier of the Cross	Isaac Watts
Amazing Grace	John Newton
And Can It Be	Charles Wesley
Angels from the Realms of Glory	James Montgomery
Angels We Have Heard on High	James Chadwick
Arise, My Soul, Arise	Charles Wesley
At Even, Ere the Sun Was Set	Henry Twells

At the Cross	Isaac Watts
At the Name of Jesus	Caroline Maria Noel
Awake My Soul, and with the Sun	Thomas Ken
Away in a Manger	Unknown, 1884
Be Not Dismayed	Civilla Durfee Martin
Be Still, My Soul	Katharina Amalia von Schlegel
Be Thou My Vision	Irish Hymn
Behold the Savior of Mankind	Samuel Wesley Sr.
Behold What Manner of Love	Van Tine
Beneath the Cross of Jesus	Elizabeth Cecelia Clephane
Blessed Assurance	Fanny Crosby
Blessed Be the Name	William H. Clark
Blessing and Honor and Glory and Power	Horatius Bonar
Blest Be the Tie That Binds	John Fawcett
Break Thou the Bread of Life	Mary Artemisia Lathbury
Breathe on Me, Breath of God	Edwin Hatch
Channels Only	Mary Maxwell
Children of the Heavenly Father	Karolina Sandell-Berg
Christ Arose	Robert Lowry
Christ Is Made the Sure Foundation	Latin Hymn
Christ Jesus Lay in Death's Strong Bands	Martin Luther
Christ the Lord Is Risen Today	Charles Wesley
Close to Thee	Fanny Crosby
Come, Holy Spirit, Dove Divine	Adoniram Judson
Come, Holy Spirit, Heavenly Dove	Isaac Watts
Come, Thou Almighty King	Unknown, 1757
Come, Thou Fount of Every Blessing	Robert Robinson
Come, Thou Long-Expected Jesus	Charles Wesley
Come, We That Love the Lord	Isaac Watts

Come, Ye Thankful People, Come	Henry Alford
Comfort, Comfort Ye My People	Johannes Olearius
Crown Him with Many Crowns	Matthew Bridges
Day by Day With Each Passing Moment	Karolina Sandell-Berg
Day is Daying in the West	Mary Artemisia Lathbury
Fairest Lord Jesus	Munster Gesangbuch
Faith of Our Fathers	Frederick William Faber
For All the Saints	William Walsham How
For the Beauty of the Earth	Folliot Sanford Pierpoint
From Greenland's Icy Mountains	Reginald Heber
Gentle Jesus, Meek and Mild	Charles Wesley
Give of Your Best to the Master	Howard Benjamin Grose
Glorious Things of Thee Are Spoken	John Newton
Go Tell It on the Mountain	John Work and Don Hustad
Go to Dark Gethsemane	James Montgomery
God Moves in a Mysterious Way	William Cowper
God of Our Fathers	Daniel Crane Roberts
God Rest Ye Merry, Gentlemen	Unknown
Good Christian Men, Rejoice	Heinrich Suso
Grace Greater than Our Sin	Julia Harriette Johnston
Grace, 'Tis a Charming Sound	Philip Doddridge
Great Is Thy Faithfulness	Thomas Obediah Chisholm
Guide Me, O Thou Great Jehovah	William Williams
Hallelujah Chorus	Handel
Hallelujah, What a Savior	Philip Paul Bliss
Hark! A Thrilling Voice Is Sounding	Latin Hymn
Hark! The Herald Angels Sing	Charles Wesley
Have Thine Own Way, Lord	Adelaide Addison Pollard
His Name is Wonderful	A. Meir

Holy, Holy, Holy	Reginald Heber
How Firm a Foundation	Unknown, 1787
How Great Thou Art	Carl Boberg
How Lovely Is Thy Dwelling Place	Scottish Psalter
How Sweet the Name of Jesus Sounds	John Newton
I Am Not Skilled to Understand	Dorothy Greenwell
I Am Thine, O Lord	Fanny Crosby
I Have Decided to Follow Jesus	Unknown
I Heard the Voice of Jesus Say	Horatius Bonar
I Know That My Redeemer Lives	Samuel Medley
I Know Whom I Have Believed	Daniel Webster Whittle
I Love to Tell the Story	Arabella Katherine Hankey
I Need Thee Every Hour	Annie Sherwood Hawks
I Sing the Mighty Power of God	Isaac Watts
I Surrender All	Judson W. Van de Venter
I Will Sing of My Redeemer	Philip Paul Bliss
I Will Sing the Wondrous Story	Francis Harold Rowley
In Christ There Is No East or West	John Oxenham, pseudonym of William A. Dunkerley
In the Cross of Christ I Glory	John Bowring
It Came upon the Midnight Clear	Edmund Hamilton Sears
It Is Well with My Soul	Horatio Gates Spafford
I've Found a Friend, O Such a Friend	James Grindlay Small
Jesus Calls Us	Cecil Francis Alexander
Jesus Christ Is Risen Today	Latin Hymn
Jesus Loves Me	Anna Bartlett Warner
Jesus Paid It All	Elvina Mabel Hall
Jesus Shall Reign	Isaac Watts
Jesus! What a Friend for Sinners	J. Wilbur Chapman

Jesus, I Am Resting, Resting	Jean Sophia Pigott
Jesus, I My Cross Have Taken	Henry Francis Lyte
Jesus, Keep Me Near the Cross	Fanny Crosby
Jesus, Lover of My Soul	Charles Wesley
Jesus, the Very Thought of Thee	Bernard of Clairvaux
Jesus, Thou Joy of Loving Hearts	Bernard of Clairvaux
Joy to the World	Isaac Watts
Joyful, Joyful, We Adore Thee	Henry Van Dyke
Just as I Am	Charlotte Elliott
Lead on, O King Eternal	Ernest Warbuton Shurtleff
Lead, Kindly Light	John Henry Newman
Leaning on the Everlasting Arms	Elisha Albright Hoffman
Let Us Break Bread Together	A Spiritual
Like A River Glorious	Frances Ridley Havergal
Living for Jesus	Thomas O. Chisholm
Lord, I'm Coming Home	William J. Kirkpatrick
Lord, Speak to Me	Frances Ridley Havergal
Love Divine, All Love Excelling	Charles Wesley
Love Lifted Me	James Rowe
Man of Sorrows	Philip Paul Bliss
More about Jesus	Eliza Edmunds Hewitt
More Love to Thee, O Christ	Elizabeth Payson Prentiss
My Faith Has Found a Resting Place	Lidie H. Edmunds, pseudonym of Eliza Edmunds Hewitt
My Faith Looks Up to Thee	Ray Palmer
My Hope Is Built on Nothing Less	Edward Mote
My Jesus, I Love Thee	William Ralph Featherston
Near the Cross	Fanny Crosby
Near to the Heart of God	Cleland Boyd McAfee

Nearer, My God, to Thee	Sarah Flower Adams
Now Thank We All Our God	Martin Rinkart
Now the Day Is Over	Sabine Baring-Gould
O Come All Ye Faithful	John F. Wade
O for a Closer Walk with God	William Cowper
O for a Thousand Tongues to Sing	Charles Wesley
O God, Our Help in Ages Past	Isaac Watts
O Jesus, I Have Promised	John Ernest Bode
O Little Town of Bethlehem	Phillips Brooks
O Love That Wilt Not Let Me Go	George Matheson
O Master, Let Me Walk with Thee	Washington Gladden
O Sacred Head, Now Wounded	Bernard of Clairvaux
O the Deep, Deep Love of Jesus	Samuel Trevor Francis
O Worship the King	Robert Grant
O Zion, Haste	Mary Ann Thomson
Once in Royal David's City	Cecil Francis Alexander
Onward, Christian Soldiers	Sabine Baring-Gould
Open My Eyes, That I May See	Clara H. Scott
Praise Him! Praise Him!	Fanny Crosby
Praise, My Soul, the King of Heaven	Henry Francis Lyte
Prayer Is the Soul's Sincere Desire	James Montgomery
Redeemed, and with the Price of Blood	Fanny Crosby
Redeemed, How I Love to Proclaim It	Fanny Crosby
Rescue the Perishing	Fanny Crosby
Revive Us Again	William Paton Mackay
Rise Up, O Men of God	William Pearson Merrill
Rock of Ages	Augustus M. Toplady
Savior, Like a Shepherd Lead Us	Dorothy A. Thrupp
Search Me, O God	J. Edwin Orr
Silent Night, Holy Night	Josef Mohr

Softly and Tenderly Jesus Is Calling	Will Lamartine Thompson
Spirit of God, Descend upon My Heart	George Croly
Stand Up, Stand Up for Jesus	George Duffield Jr.
Standing on the Promises	R. Kelso Carter
Sweet Hour of Prayer	William W. Walford
Take My Life and Let It Be	Frances Ridley Havergal
Take the Name of Jesus with You	Lydia O. Baxter
Take Time to Be Holy	William Dunn Longstaff
Tell Me the Old Old Story	Arabella Katherine Hankey
Tell Me the Story of Jesus	Fanny Crosby
The Church's One Foundation	Samuel John Stone
The First Noel	English Carol, 1833
The King of Love My Shepherd Is	Henry William Baker
The Old Rugged Cross	George Bennard
The Strife Is O'er	Latin Hymn
There Is a Balm in Gilead	A Spiritual
There Is a Fountain Filled with Blood	William Cowper
There Is a Green Hill Far Away	Cecil Francis Alexander
There Shall Be Showers of Blessing	Daniel W. White
There's a Wideness in God's Mercy	Frederick William Faber
This Is My Father's World	Maltbie Davenport Babcock
'Tis So Sweet to Trust in Jesus	Louisa M. R. Stead
To God Be the Glory	Fanny Crosby
Trust and Obey	John H. Sammis
Turn Your Eyes upon Jesus	Helen Howarth Lemmel
Under His Wings I Am Safely Abiding	William Orcutt Cushing
We Plow the Fields	Matthias Claudius
We Praise Thee, O God, Our Redeemer, Creator	Julia Bulkley Cady Cory
We Three Kings of Orient Are	John Henry Hopkins, Jr.

We're Marching to Zion	Isaac Watts
Were You There	A Spiritual
We've a Story to Tell to the Nations	H. Ernest Nichol
What a Friend We Have in Jesus	Joseph Medlicott Scriven
What Child Is This	William Chatterton Dix
When I Survey the Wondrous Cross	Isaac Watts
When Morning Gilds the Skies	German Hymn
When We All Get to Heaven	Eliza Edmunds Hewitt
While Shepherds Watched Their Flocks	Nahum Tate
Who Is on the Lord's Side	Frances Ridley Havergal
Wonderful Grace of Jesus	Haldor Lillenas
Ye Servants of God	Charles Wesley

Selected Bibliography

Abraham, Gerald. *The Concise Oxford History of Music.* London/New York: Oxford University Press, 1979.

Abraham, Gerald, ed. *The History of Music in Sound.* 10 vols. London: Oxford University Press, 1953–1957.

Achtemeier, Paul J., gen. ed. *Harper's Bible Dictionary.* San Francisco: Harper & Row, Publishers, 1985.

Bromiley, Geoffrey W. "History of New Testament Worship." Pages 101–10 in *The Biblical Foundations of Christian Worship.* Vol. 1 of *The Complete Library of Christian Worship.* Edited by Robert E. Webber. 7 vols. Peabody, Mass.: Hendrickson, 1995.

Clarke, Adam. *The Holy Bible, Containing the Old and New Testaments, the Text Carefully Printed from the Most Correct Copies of the Present Authorized Translation, Including the Marginal Readings and Parallel Texts: With a Commentary and Critical Notes Designed as a Help to a Better Understanding of the Sacred Writings.* 3d ed. New York: Hitt & Paul, 1817–1825.

Crim, Keith, gen. ed. *The Perennial Dictionary of World Religions.* San Francisco: Harper & Row, Publishers, 1981.

Douglas, J. D., ed. *The New International Dictionary of the Christian Church.* Rev. ed. Grand Rapids, Mich.: Zondervan, 1974.

Dowley, Tim, ed. *Eerdmans' Handbook to the History of Christianity.* Grand Rapids, Mich.: Eerdmans, 1977.

Engel, Carl. *Music of the Most Ancient Nations, Particularly of the Assyrians, Egyptians, and Hebrews; with Special Reference to Recent Discoveries in Western Asia and in Egypt.* 8 vols. Rev. ed. London: William Reeves, 1929.

Ferguson, Donald N. *A History of Musical Thought.* New York: F. S. Crofts & Co., 1935.

Fillmore, John C. *Lessons in Musical History,* Philadelphia: T. Presser, 1888.

Galpin, Francis W. *The Music of the Sumerians and Their Immediate Successors, the Babylonians, and Assyrians, Described and Illustrated from Original Sources.* Cambridge: The University Press, 1937.

Kerr, Phillip. *Music in Evangelism, and Stories of Famous Christian Songs.* Glendale, Calif.: Gospel Music Publishers, 1954.

Lane, Edward W. *An Account of the Manners and Customs of the Modern Egyptians, Written in Egypt During the Years 1833, 1834, and 1835, Partly from Notes Made During a Former Visit to That Country in the Years 1825, 1826, 1827, and 1828.* 5th ed. London: J. Murray, 1860.

Layard, Austen H. *Discoveries Among the Ruins of Nineveh and Babylon; with Travels in Armenia, Kurdistan, and the Desert: Being the Result of a Second Expedition Undertaken for the Trustees of the British Museum.* New York: Harper & Brothers, 1853.

Lockyer, Herbert Sr. *All the Trades and Occupations of the Bible.* Grand Rapids, Mich.: Zondervan, 1969.

Maus, Cynthia P. *Christ and the Fine Arts; an Anthology of Pictures, Poetry, Music, and Stories Centering in the Life of Christ.* 5th ed. New York/London: Harper & Brothers, 1938.

McGuckin, John A. *At the Lighting of the Lamps: Hymns of the Ancient Church.* Harrisburg, Penn.: Morehouse, 1995.

Millar, James. "Music." Pages 2094–101 in vol. 3 of *The International Standard Bible Encyclopedia.* Edited by James Orr. 4 vols. 1939. Repr., Peabody, Mass.: Hendrickson, 1994.

Olson, Lee G. "Music and the Musical Instruments of the Bible." Pages 562–66 of *Zondervan's Pictorial Bible Dictionary.* Edited by Merrill C. Tenney. Grand Rapids, Mich.: Zondervan, 1967.

Rawlinson, George. *The Five Great Monarchies of the Ancient Eastern World; or, the History, Geography, and Antiquities of Chaldaea, Assyria, Babylon, Media, and Persia, Collected and Illustrated from Ancient and Modern Sources.* 4 vols. London: J. Murray, 1862–1867.

Sharpe, Samuel. *Egyptian Mythology and Egyptian Christianity: With Their Influence on the Opinions of Modern Christendom*. London: J. R. Smith, 1863.

Sollberger, Edmond. *The Babylonian Legend of the Flood*. London: Trustees of the British Museum, 1962.

Spurgeon, C. H. "Psalm 92." Pages 116–33 in *Psalms 58–110*. Vol. 2 of *The Treasury of David Containing an Original Exposition of the Book of Psalms*. Repr., Peabody, Mass.: Hendrickson, 1988.

Stainer, John. *The Music of the Bible: With Some Account of the Development of Modern Musical Instruments from Ancient Types*. 2d ed. London: Novello/New York: H. W. Gray, 1914.

Ulrich, Homer, and Paul A. Pisk. *A History of Music and Musical Style*. New York: Harcourt, Brace & World, 1963.

Werner, Eric. *The Sacred Bridge: The Interdependence of Liturgy and Music in Synagogue and Church During the First Millennium*. 2 vols. London: D. Dobson/New York: Columbia University Press, 1959. Repr., London: D. Dobson/New York: Columbia University Press, 1984.

Wilson-Dickson, Andrew. *A Brief History of Christian Music: From Biblical Times to the Present*. Oxford: Lion, 1997.

Wilson-Dickson, Andrew. *The Story of Christian Music: From Gregorian Chant to Black Gospel: An Authoritative Illustrated Guide to All the Major Traditions of Music for Worship*. Minneapolis: Augsburg Fortress, 1996.